1997–98 Annual Supplement to

THE PIANO BOOK

BUYING & OWNING A NEW OR USED PIANO

LARRY FINE

BROOKSIDE PRESS • BOSTON, MASSACHUSETTS

Brookside Press
P.O. Box 178, Jamaica Plain, Massachusetts 02130
(617) 522-7182
(800) 545-2022 (orders)

e-mail: pianobk@tiac.net
world wide web: http://www.tiac.net/users/pianobk

1997–98 Annual Supplement to The Piano Book copyright © 1997 by Lawrence Fine

Printed in the United States of America

ISBN 0-9617512-8-2

NOTICE

Reasonable efforts have been made to secure accurate information for this publication. Due in part to the fact that manufacturers and distributors will not always willingly make this information available, however, some indirect sources have been relied upon.

Neither the author nor publisher make any guarantees with respect to the accuracy of the information contained herein and will not be liable for damages—incidental, consequential, or otherwise—resulting from the use of the information.

INTRODUCTION

This is the second issue of a publication I expect to publish annually each August. Because of the long time span between successive editions of *The Piano Book*, it is impractical to provide in the book itself the detailed model and price data that price-conscious shoppers increasingly seek. Similarly, updated information about manufacturers and products is needed in a timely manner. I hope this modest companion volume will effectively extend the "shelf life" of *The Piano Book* as a valuable reference work, as well as serve as an additional information resource for piano buyers and piano lovers.

Larry Fine

June, 1997

CONTENTS

MANUFACTURER and PRODUCT UPDATE

This section describes changes to companies, products, and brand names since the third edition of *The Piano Book* went to press in late 1994. The listings are cumulative; that is, where still relevant, information contained in last year's *Supplement* has been retained, and changes that have occurred during the past year have been added. It is not intended, however, that this information take the place of the reviews in *The Piano Book*. With some exceptions, this update is limited to changes of a factual nature only, whereas the book contains, in addition, critical reviews and recommendations. If a company or brand name is not listed here, it means that there is nothing new of substance to report. To correctly understand some of the price and model information listed here, I recommend that you read page 72 of *The Piano Book*.

August Förster—See "Förster, August"

Baldorr & Son—Name discontinued

Baldwin

At the time the third edition of *The Piano Book* was going to press, Baldwin was in the process of completely reorganizing its product line (and also undergoing major changes in management). The description of the new models given in the book was based on Baldwin's tentative plans at that time, but the plans changed and the actual product line turned out a little differently.

Baldwin also owns the **Wurlitzer** and **Chickering** trade names. In its reorganized product line, the Wurlitzers represent the lower-priced pianos, the Chickerings the mid-priced American-made grands, and the Baldwins the mid- to upper-level verticals and high-end grands. All are sold by the same dealer network. (In the past, Wurlitzer and Baldwin/Chickering had separate dealer networks, and the Baldwin line included instruments at all price levels, which tended to confuse customers about the relative value of the Baldwin name.)

In the new Baldwin line, the spinet model has been discontinued. The console, 43-1/2" in height, comes in three basic model types. All three use the same back and action, but differ in cabinetry. The model E100 is the console with a continental-style cabinet. It has a slightly longer key length and deeper cabinet than the continental-style model it replaces. The model 660 series console is a furniture-style model known as the "Classic". However, unlike the lesser "Classic" model it replaces, this one has Baldwin's 19-ply pinblock, full-size action, and solid spruce soundboard. The upper-level console, the model 2090 series, is called the "Acrosonic", a name Baldwin has traditionally used for its upper-level consoles and spinets. This model series has fancier cabinet features and hardware than the Classic, but is the same instrument inside.

Baldwin 45" studio verticals, still known as the "Hamilton", come in three model types. The model 243HPA is the school studio. Its functional-looking cabinet has been redesigned to provide easier access for servicing, as well as for other practical reasons. The model 5050 series studio, known as the "Limited Edition", is the fancy-looking studio. It is made in only three furniture styles, each limited to a production run of one thousand instruments, after which the style is changed. The model E250 is the studio in a contemporary cabinet style. The model 248, a 48" "Professional Upright", introduced in 1997, contains many interesting new technical features aimed primarily at enhancing tuning stability and evenness of tone. The model 6000 52" "Concert Vertical" upright remains the same.

The Baldwin "Artist" series of grand pianos remains substantially the same, with the following small changes: each piano now comes with an adjustable Artist bench; the sharps are now made of solid ebony wood instead of plastic; the weight characteristics of the action have been changed to reduce inertia; and a 5' 8" Louis XVI style (model 227) has been added to the line.

The Chickering line of American-made grands is new. The two models, 4' 10" (model 410) and 5' 7" (model 507), are adapted from the troublesome Classic line of Baldwin grands that was discontinued at the end of 1994. According to Baldwin, the new models have been redesigned and structurally enhanced.

The Wurlitzer vertical piano line is now limited to a 37" spinet and an entry-level 42" console with a compressed action. All other Wurlitzer consoles, studios, and uprights, both American-made and Korean-made, have been discontinued, since they would otherwise compete with the Baldwin line. The Wurlitzer 5' grand (model G550) and all Wurlitzer grands made by Young Chang have been discontinued. All grands with the Wurlitzer name are now made by Samick (4' 7", 5' 1", and 5' 7") and are the same as the grands formerly bearing the name "D.H. Baldwin", a name which is no longer being used.

New in 1997 is Baldwin's ConcertMaster electronic player piano system. ConcertMaster utilizes the playback mechanism from the QRS Pianomation system (see under "QRS/Pianomation" in *The Piano Book*) and comes with a floppy disk drive, a compact disc (CD) drive, and a 540-megabyte hard drive pre-loaded with 20 hours of music. The floppy disk drive can read just about any type of General MIDI music software on the market, including those from the Yamaha Disklavier and PianoDisc systems. The CD drive can read the QRS CDs containing analog audio accompaniment. The hard drive has a capacity of 10,000 songs, which can be input from any MIDI source, including computer disks, the internet, and so forth. A "Performance option" adds recording capabilities and turns the piano into a MIDI controller, complete with velocity sensitivity, assignable split point, and other features (see under "Gulbransen" in *The Piano Book* for further explanation of this type of system). ConcertMaster can be operated via a wireless remote, included.

ConcertMaster comes factory-installed on select models of Baldwin, Wurlitzer, and Chickering pianos, and can be special-ordered or field-installed into any Baldwin product. The playback unit, installed, adds about $9,000 to the list price of a piano, the Performance option an additional $1,300. (The usual discounts apply, especially as an incentive to purchase the piano.)

Bechner—Name discontinued

Becker, J.

New importer/distributor:

Bellville & Sons
115 Bellam Blvd.
San Rafael, California 94901

415-456-5314
800-825-1447

Distribution of this brand in the U.S. has been temporarily curtailed because of a supply shortage.

Belarus—Name discontinued. See "Schubert"

Betting, Th.—Name discontinued. See "Schirmer & Son"

Blüthner

A 6' 1" grand, called "Haessler", has been added to the Blüthner product line. (Haessler is a Blüthner family name.) This model is more conventional in many of its technical and cosmetic features than the regular models and costs about twenty-five percent less. For example, it is loop-strung instead of single-strung; omits the "aliquot" strings (fourth string per note); and has normal, straight-cut, angle-mounted hammers. Case and plate cosmetics are simpler.

Boston

A 5' 1" grand has been added to the line.

Chickering—See "Baldwin"

Disklavier—See "Yamaha"

Dobbert, Fritz (new listing)

Bellville & Sons
115 Bellam Blvd.
San Rafael, California 94901

415-456-5314
800-825-1447

These pianos are manufactured in Brazil and made their debut in the U.S. a few years ago. Importation has been temporarily curtailed because of an unfavorable currency exchange rate.

Estonia

A 5' 4" grand model has been added to the line. The 9' concert grand comes with a Renner action; the 5' 4" and 6' 3" grands are available with Renner actions, in addition to the standard models with Schwander actions.

Correction to historical information: The Tallinn Piano Factory was founded in 1893 by Ernst Hiis under his own name. Around 1950, the government of Estonia consolidated many smaller Estonian piano makers into the Hiis factory under the Tallinn name. This factory focuses primarily on making grand pianos and says that it is the largest maker of grands among Scandinavian countries and Eastern Europe.

Falcone—See "Mason & Hamlin"

Fandrich

New address:

Fandrich Piano Co., Inc.
P.O. Box 961
South Haven, Michigan 49090

312-427-4200

The original U.S.-made Fandrich upright piano, previously from Washington state, is now being built in Michigan. Actions are manufactured by Renner in Germany using the Fandrich Vertical Action™ design and assembled in the U.S. (Do not confuse this piano with the Chinese-made Fandrich & Sons piano described below.)

Fandrich & Sons (new listing)

Fandrich & Sons Pianos
12515 Lake City Way, NE
Seattle, Washington 98125

206-361-1221

Fandrich & Sons pianos are sold by the people who invented the Fandrich Vertical Action™. The pianos are made in China by the Guangzhou Piano Manufactory, the same company that makes Pearl River pianos. Fandrich & Sons makes extensive modifications and improvements to the piano in the U.S. and then assembles and installs the Fandrich Vertical Action™ from a combination of Chinese, American, and German (Renner) parts. The piano is also available with a standard Chinese-made action. At present, these pianos are sold primarily in the Seattle area. (Do not confuse these pianos with the original U.S.-made Fandrich piano described under "Fandrich" above.)

Price range: With Fandrich action (51" only) — $9,250; with standard action (46" and 51") — $4,200–4,700.

Warranty: Twelve years, parts and labor

Models: 46" studio, 51" upright

Feurich

New importer/distributor:

Schimmel Piano Corp.
251 Memorial Drive
Lititz, Pennsylvania 17543

800-426-3205

Feurich grands are now being manufactured by Schimmel. They are identical in most respects to Schimmel grands of the same size, except that the Feurichs benefit from the use of Kluge keys with artificial-ivory keytops, as well as some cosmetic changes to the cabinet.

Förster, August

New importer/distributor address:

German American Trading Co.
13540 N. Florida Ave.
Tampa, Florida 33613

813-961-8405

Fritz Dobbert—See "Dobbert, Fritz"

Grinnell Bros.—See "Samick / Kohler & Campbell"

Grotrian

New importer/distributor:

Strings Limited
314 S. Milwaukee Ave., Ste. B
Libertyville, Illinois 60048

847-367-5224

Hastings—Name discontinued

Hazelton—See "Samick / Kohler & Campbell"

Ibach

Soon after the third edition of *The Piano Book* went to press, Daewoo decided not to distribute Korean-made Ibach pianos in the U.S. However, the pianos *are* being distributed in Canada. The Canadian distributor is:

Bingley Distributors
280 Dufferin Ave.
Trenton, Ontario
Canada K8V 5G2

613-394-4729

Jasper (-American)—See "Kimball"

Kawai

Kawai has made extensive changes to its product line in the few years since the third edition of *The Piano Book* was published. As is characteristic of Kawai, the vertical piano line—the console models in particular—can be confusing. Briefly, Kawai's console line consists of the 500- and 600-series pianos in furniture-style cabinets and the CX-5 series in continental style. Earlier the 502, and now the 503, are 42" consoles in simple furniture styles. The CX-5 (sometimes called CX-5N) is the same piano in continental style, without casters and therefore only 41" tall. The 602, no longer made, was a fancier-looking version of the 502. The model 603 was enlarged to 44" and then redesigned as a distinct scale in model 604. The well-respected Japanese-made console model CE-11 has been discontinued.

Kawai's least expensive piano at present is the very popular model CX-5H, a 45" piano that Kawai calls a "studio". This model actually has the same scale design as the 41" model CX-5 console, but the height has been increased to 45" through the use of casters and an extended back. Also like the CX-5, this model has the compressed action typical of a console piano (see page 44 of *The Piano Book* for further explanation). In other words, the model CX-5H is essentially a console piano in a studio-size cabinet. Although the extra height may be appealing to some customers, it confers no technical or musical advantage (nor disadvantage). The CX-5H is much less expensively constructed than the CX-5, including a laminated mahogany-core soundboard and a less robust back structure. A new variant, model 504, is the same piano in a furniture-style cabinet, but with a shorter, 43" back. These inexpensive models are satisfactory entry-level pianos, but for the reasons mentioned, they may not be quite the bargain they seem initially and are probably not appropriate for more demanding applications, especially if the piano needs to be moved frequently.

Kawai's line of studio and upright pianos remains about the same as described in *The Piano Book*. The AnyTime (hybrid digital/acoustic) piano is now available in both the model CX-21 (AT-120) and the model NS-20A (AT-170).

Kawai has replaced its entire KG and GS series of grands (with the exception of the GS-100) with a new RX series. According to the company, these new pianos have NEOTEX™ keytops (Kawai's brand of ivory substitute), new case beam and plate strut configurations, a scratch-resistant music desk, and new scale designs. The "R" (Artisan Select) series of grands has essentially been phased out, except for the superior model RX-A. (Note that the "R" series mentioned in *The Piano Book* is not the same as the "RX" series; the only point of overlap is the RX-A.) A variant of the popular 5' 10" model RX-2, the RX-2S, has softer hammers with heavier moldings, resulting in a mellower tone. A 7' 6" model RX-7 is due to be released in late 1997. Some recent technical changes to the grands include vertically-laminated bridges with bridge caps, a harder inner rim, and more extensive use of ABS Styran in grand action parts.

In other changes, the new model GM-2 is an inexpensive 5' grand with a very scaled-down cabinet, including an almost primitive-looking, but functional, pedal lyre. A new model GE-1A is the same as the model GE-1, with the addition of a duplex scale. The 5' 9" model GE-3 grand has replaced the 5' 7" GE-2. To celebrate the company's 70th anniversary, in 1997 Kawai is making some of its models, both grand and vertical, available with enhancements. Most of the enhancements are cosmetic, but a few, such as a Soft-Fall fallboard or scratch-resistant music desk, are functional. These models are marked "Limited Edition" (LE).

Correction: *The Piano Book* is incorrect in stating that the Kawai warranty does not cover broken strings. As with most other brands, string breakage is covered except when due to extremely heavy use or abuse.

Kimball

In February 1996, Kimball announced that it would cease all production of vertical pianos. This completes Kimball's exit from the domestic piano business. In July 1995, Kimball stopped making grands, and for a year or so

Kimball verticals were largely built by Baldwin, with only cabinets and final assembly by Kimball. Kimball will continue to honor its warranties, and will also continue to build piano cabinets for other makers, such as Samick and Kawai, as it has for some time now. The company sold most of its piano-making equipment to a Chinese piano manufacturer, with whom, reportedly, it hopes to develop a joint venture in the Chinese market. Kimball International's Bösendorfer division is unaffected by these changes. The Herrburger Brooks division has been sold, but its actions and action parts are still being manufactured in England as before.

Knabe (new listing)

Music Systems Research
4111-A North Freeway Blvd.
Sacramento, California 95834

800-566-3472
916-567-9999

The "PianoDisc" line of pianos previously offered by Music Systems Research (MSR) has been discontinued and replaced by a new line of pianos resurrecting the Knabe name. The piano's cabinet design and appearance have been altered, and the hammers have been changed, resulting in different touch characteristics, the company says. The keybeds are modified at the factory for easier installation of a PianoDisc system at a later date, if desired. All Knabe pianos are extensively serviced in MSR's California facility prior to being shipped to dealers. Like the discontinued PianoDisc line, Knabe is made by Young Chang in Korea.

Knabe pianos can be ordered by the dealer as regular acoustic pianos, or with the PianoDisc or GT-360 QuietTime systems factory-installed. See under "PianoDisc" in *The Piano Book* and in this *Supplement* for more information on these systems.

Knight

Corrected address and phone:

Alfred Knight Ltd.
154 Clapham Park Road
London SW4 7DE England

(44) 71 978 2444

Kohler & Campbell—See "Samick / Kohler & Campbell"

Maddison (new listing)

North American Piano Group
P.O. Box 14128
Bradenton, Florida 34280

800-336-9164

This piano is made by the Guangzhou Piano Manufactory in Guangzhou, China, the same factory that makes the Pearl River piano.

Mason & Hamlin

New phone number: 508-374-8888

In mid-1994, the Mason & Hamlin Companies ceased production of all Mason & Hamlin, Falcone, and Sohmer pianos, and in January 1995 filed for Chapter 7 (liquidation) bankruptcy. Shortly thereafter, a Boston-based piano rebuilding firm, Premier Pianos, obtained the controlling interest in the company from its former owner and persuaded the Bankruptcy Court to change the bankruptcy filing to Chapter 11 (reorganization).

From early 1995 to early 1996, the new owners completed the manufacture of pianos left unfinished when the plant closed, made some new pianos from scratch, and attempted to fight off legal attempts by creditors to force liquidation of the company or its sale to another party. (Many creditors did not have faith in the new owners' ability to put the company back on its feet.) On April 5, 1996, the Court sided with the creditors and approved the sale of Mason & Hamlin to Kirk and Gary Burgett, owners of Music Systems Research, manufacturer of the PianoDisc electronic player piano systems. The Mason & Hamlin assets also included the Falcone, Sohmer, Knabe, and George Steck brand names and designs.

At the time of this writing, the Burgett brothers are manufacturing Mason & Hamlin pianos once again at the Haverhill, Massachusetts factory to, they say, the original high standards. They are making the 50" vertical, as well as the models A and BB grands. Initial reports on these instruments are positive. The Knabe name is being applied to a line of pianos from Korea (see "Knabe"). Some of the Mason & Hamlins and many of the Knabes are being sold with PianoDisc units installed. Plans for the Falcone, Sohmer, and George Steck brand names are still being discussed.

For those who have a need to know, the serial numbers of the Mason & Hamlin pianos built or completed by the interim (Premier) ownership were from 90590 to 90613 inclusive.

Nakamichi / Nakamura

Due to a trademark conflict with the Nakamichi company that sells audio equipment, the Nakamichi piano (no relation) now goes by the name Nakamura.

Niemeyer (new listing)

North American Music
126 Rt. 303
W. Nyack, New York 10994

914-353-3520
800-541-2331

These pianos are made in China by the Dongbei Piano Co.

Pearl River (new listing)

New distributor:

Poppenberg & Associates
966 S. Pearl St.
Denver, Colorado 80209

303-765-5775

These pianos are made by the Guangzhou Piano Manufactory in Guangzhou, China, the largest piano factory in China and one of the largest in the world. This is a return of the Pearl River name, which was present in the U.S. market several years ago, but discontinued because the quality at that time was not good enough to allow the brand to maintain a foothold in the market. With the influx of investment by the Chinese government and foreign businesses, the quality has greatly improved and continues to improve rapidly.

Petrof / Weinbach

Petrof now has a 52" upright with a Renner action, not available under the Weinbach label.

The 6' 4" model III Petrof grand (but not Weinbach) now uses Renner action parts, though not a complete Renner action. The parts are assembled onto a Petrof action frame at the Petrof factory. The 7' 9" and 9' 3" models have complete Renner actions. However, a new 6' 4" model III-M, made in the same factory as the two larger models, does have a complete Renner action, as well as other refinements common to the larger models.

Petrof has switched from Delignit to a 7-ply beech pinblock in its Petrof and Weinbach grands.

PianoDisc

The parent company is now called Music Systems Research. The PianoDisc line of pianos has been discontinued and replaced with the Knabe line. See "Knabe".

Concerning the PianoDisc player piano systems, the new model "PDS 128 Plus" plays both floppy disks and their specialized PianoCD software. The unit has a floppy disk drive, and by attaching a CD player you can play the PianoCDs from the same control unit. One channel of the PianoCD contains the digital information that operates the piano playback, while the other channel contains actual audio vocals and accompaniment that play through your speakers. Options still include TFT MIDI Record, the Symphony Sound Module, and amplified speakers, as well as the PianoMute Rail from the new QuietTime system (see below) to "turn off" the acoustic piano sound if desired. The less-expensive "PianoCD" system is available, without a floppy disk drive, for those customers who desire to play only PianoCDs. Both systems feature a full dynamic range of 127 levels of expression.

The latest version of the PDS 128 Plus incorporates new "SilentDrive" technology, circuitry that allows much closer control of the key and pedal solenoids. The new units are said to operate more quietly, and to provide better volume control and faster key and pedal response than before. The system is now compatible with virtually all Standard MIDI file software.

"QuietTime" is Music Systems Research's newest system. QuietTime turns a piano into a hybrid acoustic/digital instrument. In regular mode, the piano plays just like an ordinary piano. If desired, the system will provide orchestrated accompaniment through amplified speakers. When the QuietTime feature is activated, the acoustic sound is turned off (the PianoMute rail prevents the hammers from hitting the strings) and the digital piano and other instrumental sounds are turned on and can be listened to using

16

stereo headphones (perfect for late-night playing). Two headphone jacks are supplied. Like the PianoDisc system, QuietTime can be installed into just about any piano.

The QuietTime model GT-360 supplies 128 different General MIDI instrumental sounds, MIDI In, Out & Thru, 16 MIDI channels with reverb and other effects, key range settings, and the ability to create and save up to 75 of your own custom sound-combination presets. The less expensive model GT-90 has 16 instrumental selections which are factory pre-set, and the ability to make 40 possible sound combinations. The emphasis on this model is simplicity of operation, as most functions can be accessed by pushing one or two buttons.

For price information, see the Model and Pricing Guide section of this *Supplement* under "PianoDisc".

QRS / Pianomation

The Pianomation system can now be configured in a variety of ways. As before, the customer can use his or her own regular CD player, which can be controlled with an optional wireless remote. QRS also now makes a more sophisticated CD-ROM drive that fits under the keybed of the piano. If desired, the unit can be purchased with a 3.5" floppy disk drive instead of, or in addition to, the CD-ROM drive. (The units that fit under the keybed cannot at present be controlled with the wireless remote.) The floppy disk drive can read Standard MIDI files and so is compatible with virtually all music software on the market, including software made for the Yamaha Disklavier and for PianoDisc.

As before, Pianomation is available with Orchestration and Record options. When a Pianomation CD is played with the Orchestration option, one channel of the CD contains the digital information that operates the piano playback, while the other channel contains actual audio vocals and accompaniment that play through your speakers. The Pianomation CD library includes live recordings of major symphony orchestras as accompaniment for the piano. The processor has been upgraded to generate a greater range of expression from the number of expression levels available from the CDs. A new optically-sensing version of the Record option will be available in Fall 1997.

QRS offers a version of Pianomation called "Playola", which sits atop the keys (like the "Vorsetzer" of the player piano's halcyon days) and plays the

17

keys with little rubber fingers, either alone or accompanied by orchestral music. Unlike Pianomation, Playola does not operate the pedals. Instead, quasi-pedal ("Magic Pedal") information is incorporated into the software and simulates the pedals through the control of note duration. This simulation is not as realistic as actually controlling the damper pedal, but should probably be sufficient for simpler applications. Playola comes with a carrying case and does not require professional installation by a technician.

For price information on Pianomation and Playola systems, see the Model and Pricing Guide section of this *Supplement* under "QRS / Pianomation".

New in 1997 is a product called "Presto-Digitation" that turns an old upright into a digital piano. A technician removes the old keys and action and replaces them with a kit consisting of a new keyboard, electronics, speakers, and a user interface. This may be a suitable fate for an older piano that would otherwise be discarded. The suggested retail price, including installation, is about $2,300. Installation takes about three hours.

Ridgewood (new listing)

Weber Piano Co.
40 Seaview Drive
Secaucus, New Jersey 07094

800-346-5351
201-902-0920

This name is being applied to furniture-style verticals and a 5' 2" grand made by the Guangzhou Piano Manufactory in Guangzhou, China, the same company that makes Pearl River pianos. The same grand is also sold under the "Sagenhaft" name.

Rieger-Kloss

New importer/distributor:

Weber Piano Co.
40 Seaview Drive
Secaucus, New Jersey 07094

800-346-5351
201-902-0920

The Czech company that makes Rieger-Kloss pianos has changed its name from "IFM Piana s.r.o." to "Bohemia s.r.o. Piano Co."

The Rieger-Kloss 6' 1" grand piano (model R-185) utilizes a case and plate made in Korea by Young Chang, identical to that of Young Chang's own grand of the same size. The action is made in Germany by Renner and everything else in the piano is made in the Czech Republic. All the components are assembled in the Czech Republic. Rieger-Kloss verticals still use mostly Czech components.

Sagenhaft (new listing)

Weber Piano Co.
40 Seaview Drive
Secaucus, New Jersey 07094

800-346-5351
201-902-0920

This piano name was listed under "Weber" in *The Piano Book*, but is now being given its own listing. The verticals are all made by the Chinese piano manufacturer Dongbei. The S-116 models are Nordiska designs, purchased from the Swedish company of the same name (as mentioned in the book); the other models are Dongbei's own designs. The Nordiska models are clearly the better of the two.

The Sagenhaft 5' 2" grand piano, just being introduced, is made by the Guangzhou Piano Manufactory in Guangzhou, China, the same company that makes Pearl River pianos. This grand is also being sold under the name "Ridgewood" (see listing).

Samick / Kohler & Campbell

Samick has added Kluge keys, Renner actions, and Renner or Abel hammers to its four largest grand piano models (6' 1", 6' 8", 7' 4", 9' 1") and has designated them as its "World Piano" series. According to the company, these models also receive extra pre-sale preparation in the U.S. before being shipped to dealers. In Samick's Kohler & Campbell line, the 6' 10" and 7' models are "World Pianos," though only the 7' has the full complement of features. The 6' 10" grand uses Samick keys, Renner action, and Renner hammers.

Other changes to the grand piano line include: adding a 4' 11" grand model SG-150, discontinuing the 5' 1" model, and replacing it with a 5' 3-1/2" model SG-161. The 5' 1" model remains, however, in the Kohler & Campbell line.

Samick has opened a factory in Indonesia for the production of guitars and pianos. The pianos currently being offered from Indonesia include the 43" models JS 043 in furniture style and JS 108 in continental style, and the 44" model JS 112 (briefly JS 114) in traditional style with toe blocks (KC 043, KC 108, and KC 112 in the Kohler & Campbell line). The models are all identical except for cabinetry. These Indonesian-assembled pianos combine keys, actions, hammers, and plates from Korea with soundboards and cabinets from Indonesia. The laminated soundboards are made of agatis, a wood indigenous to Indonesia also used for guitar soundboards. Pianos destined for U.S. dealers are first prepared for sale by Samick in California before being shipped to their final destination. During 1996–97, the name "Hazelton" was briefly used on a 43" console assembled in Korea using materials from the Indonesian factory. Once the new factory came fully online, the Hazelton model was discontinued.

Samick makes several private-label brands for individual dealers. A name not previously reported on in these pages is "Grinnell Bros.", a company that manufactured pianos in the midwest from 1902 to about 1960. The name is now owned and used by a Detroit-area piano dealer. Pianos bearing that name are made by Samick and are similar in features to pianos in the Kohler & Campbell line.

Last fall, Samick filed for bankruptcy protection with the Korean courts under a code similar to Chapter 11 in the U.S. Although its music operations have been profitable and its products have been in demand, several unprofitable non-music subsidiaries left Samick strapped for cash and saddled with debt. The Korean courts recently approved Samick's reorganization plan, allowing the company to sell off its non-music subsidiaries and continue in business. The manufacture of Samick pianos and their distribution in the U.S. have not been materially affected by the bankruptcy action.

Sängler & Söhne / Wieler

New importer/distributor address:

North American Music
126 Rt. 303
W. Nyack, New York 10994

914-353-3520
800-541-2331

These pianos have been made, at various time, in Belarus, Russia, or the Ukraine. Occasionally, the Sängler & Söhne name is used on a piano made in China that normally goes by the name "Niemeyer" (see under that name).

Sauter

Sauter has introduced versions of its 48" upright and 6' 1" grand with cabinets designed by the famous European designer Peter Maly.

The 7' 3" model 220 grand has some unusual features that at first glance seem to be only decorative, but turn out to be functional. Colored lines painted on the soundboard and white inlays on the tops of the dampers act as guides to musicians performing music for "prepared piano"—that is, ultra-modern music requiring the insertion of foreign objects between the strings or the plucking or striking of strings directly by the performer. The colored lines indicate to the performer where to touch the strings to produce certain harmonics. The white inlays on certain dampers indicate the location of the black keys for easier navigation around the "keyboard" when accessing the strings directly. This model reportedly had its origin as a custom-made instrument for the Paris Conservatory. When it met with approval, it was integrated into the Sauter line.

Schimmel

Schimmel has discontinued selling its 5' 1" grand. In 1997, the company introduced a new 6' grand (model 182). The scale design of this model is similar to that of Schimmel's 5' 10" grand (with some modifications), but the keys and action are from its 6' 10" grand. The slightly longer case of the new model was necessary to accommodate the longer keys of this action, which, Schimmel says, will give the new piano a more professional "feel" at the keyboard. The 5' 10" (model 174) will be gradually discontinued.

Schimmel now also makes grands under the Feurich label. They are identical in most respects to the Schimmel grands, except that the Feurichs benefit from the use of Kluge keys with artificial-ivory keytops, as well as cosmetic changes to the cabinet.

Schirmer & Son

New phone number: 800-942-5801

Schirmer & Son has added three grands to its previously all-vertical piano line—5' 4", 6' 3", and 9'. They are made by Estonia and are the same as the

21

Estonia-brand grands with the exception of some cosmetic changes requested by Schirmer.

Note that the Th. Betting piano line, which was identical to the Schirmer & Son line, has been discontinued.

Schubert (new listing)

Tri-Con Music Group
1626 North Prospect Ave. #2006
Milwaukee, Wisconsin 53202

941-953-9628
800-336-9164

This name was used for a brief period several years ago on an off-brand Korean piano. More recently, the name has appeared on pianos from several different former Soviet republics, currently on pianos from Belarus.

Seiler

The importer/distributor, formerly called Seiler America, has changed its name, address, and phone number to:

Prestige Pianos International, Inc.
7550 Slate Ridge Blvd.
Columbus, Ohio 43068

614-866-2605

Seiler's 48" and 52" uprights are now available with the optional "Super Magnet Repetition" (SMR) action, a patented feature that uses magnets to increase repetition speed. Tiny magnets are attached to certain action parts of each note. During playing, the magnets repel each other, forcing the parts to return to their rest position faster, ready for a new key stroke.

Optional on all Seiler pianos is the patented "Duo Vox" system that can turn a regular piano into a hybrid acoustic/digital instrument (similar to the Yamaha "Silent Series" pianos). A key sensor system interfaces with a sound module to provide the digitized sound of a concert grand at the touch of a button. A lever-actuated "acoustic mute" rail completely silences the piano by preventing the hammers from hitting the strings, or the regular muffler rail can be used for quiet acoustic-piano playing, if desired. Headphone jacks for private listening and MIDI ports for interfacing with peripherals are also provided.

Sohmer—See "Mason & Hamlin"

Steck, George—See "Mason & Hamlin"

Steigerman (new listing)

Steigerman Music Corp.
265 - 25th St.
West Vancouver, British Columbia
Canada V7V 4H9

604-921-6217

Steigerman pianos are made by the Yantai Longfeng Piano Co. of Yantai City, China. Yantai Longfeng is a relatively small company started about five years ago, and is outfitted with automated production equipment from Japan and Germany. Scales for the Steigerman pianos were developed by German scale designer Klaus Fenner, and some of the piano components come from Japan and Germany.

The Steigerman name is owned by Robert Loewen, a Canadian distributor. Over the last several decades, Loewen has used the Steigerman name on pianos from several manufacturers, including Yamaha and, more recently, Samick, imported into Canada. He also imports pianos from a variety of Chinese companies onto which dealers can place their own house-brand names.

At present, the Steigerman name is only being used on pianos from Yantai Longfeng and the pianos are available in both the U.S. and Canada. The line consists of 43", 45", and 48" vertical models and a 5' 6" grand. The company says that 5' 2" and 6' grand models will be available later in 1997.

Steinway & Sons

In April 1995, Steinway Musical Properties, Inc., parent corporation of Steinway & Sons, was purchased by Selmer Industries, Inc., parent corporation of The Selmer Company, a major manufacturer of band instruments. The new combined company, known as Steinway Musical Instruments, Inc., has conducted a public stock offering and is now listed on the New York Stock Exchange. Management at Steinway & Sons remains the same.

It is well known that Steinway's principal competition comes from used and rebuilt Steinways. The company has responded by reissuing old, turn-of-the-century designs, available in models L (5' 10-1/2") and B (6' 10-1/2"), a series of pianos Steinway calls "Limited Editions". The Limited Edition model issued in 1995, known as "Instrument of the Immortals", was actually an amalgam of several different Victorian-era designs, including round, "ice-cream cone" legs; an elaborately carved music desk; and raised beads on the case and around the plate holes; among other features. All examples of this model have been sold.

The 1997 release, informally known as "Sketch 390", commemorates the 200th anniversary of the birth of Steinway founder Heinrich Engelhard Steinway. Based on a 1903 design by J.B. Tiffany, only two instruments in this design were originally manufactured, one of which survives today. It was discovered when it came into the Steinway Restoration Department for rebuilding. This design features over forty feet of hand-carved moldings on the lid, case edges, and legs in "Tulip" and "Egg & Dart" patterns. Production of this model is limited to two hundred instruments in East Indian Rosewood and African Pommele, models L and B only.

Effective immediately, a "satin lustre" finish is standard on all Steinway grands in natural wood finishes (i.e., not ebony). Satin lustre is Steinway's name for a finish that is in between satin and high-polish in glossiness. Satin continues to be the standard finish for ebony pianos. At an additional cost, any piano can be special-ordered in a high-polish finish.

Steinway has released a computer CD called "An Interactive Factory Tour" containing more than one hundred photos and video clips illustrating how its instruments are made. To obtain a copy, call or visit your local Steinway dealer. Technicians can buy it from the Steinway Parts Department.

Story & Clark

Story & Clark now makes a 5' 5" grand (the "Hampton") in the U.S. This piano is unusual in that unlike most grand rims, which are made as one continuous piece bent around a form, its maple rim is made in four pieces, glued and doweled together. The piano has German Abel hammers with a Czech- and Renner-made action, and comes in several different furniture styles. A 5' American-made grand (with a continuous bent rim) is projected for Fall 1997. The 4' 7" and 5' 1" Samick-made Story & Clark grands are now available only with Pianomation systems installed. The 44" console model, called "Prelude", is made in China by the Dongbei Piano Co.

24

Strauss (new listing)

L & M International, Inc.
6452 Bresslyn Rd.
Nashville, Tennessee 37205

615-356-3686

Strauss pianos are made by the Shanghai Piano Co. in Shanghai, China. The oldest piano manufacturer in China, Shanghai was founded over a hundred years ago by the British. The name was changed to Shanghai when the Communists took over China around 1950.

Shanghai makes pianos under a number of different names. The name currently used on pianos for export to the U.S. is "Strauss". In the recent past, the name "Nieer" was sometimes used. Pianos can also be special-ordered with the name "Helios".

Walter, Charles R.

The "Janssen" line of consoles has been discontinued. The Walter 6' 4" grand is now available.

Weber

The 43" W-109 console and the 48" W-121 upright are made in Young Chang's new factory in Tianjin, China (see "Young Chang" for more details). The other Weber models are made in Young Chang's factory in Korea.

Weinbach—See "Petrof/Weinbach"

Wieler—See "Sängler & Söhne / Wieler"

Woodchester (new listing)

The Woodchester Piano Co. Ltd.
Woodchester Mills
Woodchester, Stroud
Gloucestershire GL5 5NW
England

(44) 453 872871

This English company was founded in 1994 on the site of the old Bentley piano factory, which was abandoned when Bentley was purchased by another company. Some of the old Bentley workforce continues to work for Woodchester.

Woodchester manufactures vertical pianos from 44-1/2" to 48" in height. The larger models have Renner actions, Abel hammers, Delignit pinblocks, and backs based on a Rippen design. Components for the smaller models are from Poland and the Czech Republic.

Prices range: approximately $4,000-8,000

Warranty: Five years, parts and labor

Wurlitzer—See "Baldwin"

Yamaha

In Yamaha's acoustic piano line, the models G1 and G2 (5' 3" and 5' 8") have been replaced with models C1 and C2 of the same size. The change is mostly in name; technically the new models are very similar to the old. A new 5' 3" model GP1 grand is the same as the model GH1B, but with a less expensive cabinet. Among the verticals, a new 44" model M450 is the model M500 with a less expensive cabinet. (Both the GH1B and the M500 series continue in the product line, however.)

Most Yamaha models are now available as Disklaviers, and many are available as "Silent Series" pianos. The 48" model U1 is currently the only model available with both the "silent" and Disklavier features in the same instrument.

In 1997, the Mark II Disklavier system became the Mark IIXG. The "XG" stands for "extended General MIDI" and refers to the new internal tone card that contains an enormous library of 676 voices and numerous special effects from which thousands of combinations can be created by users and programmers. Other new features of the Mark IIXG: MIDI files can be downloaded from any source and up to 1.44 megabytes (about three hours of music) can be stored on a built-in memory chip; the disk drive now reads both high-density and double-density floppy disks; the control unit's ROM is software-upgradable; and the unit can read Standard MIDI files and so is compatible with all player piano software on the market that adheres to that standard. Note that a few of Yamaha's less expensive grand Disklavier models are available as playback units only, with no recording capabilities.

Their model numbers contain the "XG", but not the "II".

Projected for late 1997 is the "Pro" line of Disklaviers, intended for use by recording studios and others with sophisticated recording requirements. The playback solenoid system on the Pro line contains a servo mechanism that continuously monitors performance. Most importantly, the unit can record and playback the release of notes as well as their attack, resulting in a musical rendition that is much more faithful to the original. The Disklavier Pro line will be available on selected grand models over six feet and will contain all the features of the present Disklavier product.

Young Chang

In 1995, Young Chang built a huge new piano factory in Tianjin, China. Unlike most other Chinese joint ventures, Young Chang chose to design and build the factory from scratch rather than try to reform an existing manufacturing facility. A Young Chang–owned plant in Tianjin has been making cast-iron plates for the company's Korean-made pianos for several years. The new Tianjin factory makes three piano models for export to the U.S.—the 43" model E-109 continental-style console, a 46" model E-118 studio, and a 48" model U-121N upright. The pianos are assembled from a Chinese back, plate, and cabinet, and a Korean-made action. The soundboard is solid Chinese spruce.

Young Chang has just issued a new version of its 6' 1" grand. The new model PG-185 has been refined and reengineered by Joseph Pramberger, formerly a Steinway technician and engineer for nearly thirty years and at one time Steinway's Vice-President of Manufacturing. Although the new model uses the same scale design as the older G-185, the bridges, soundboard, and hammers have been redesigned. Additionally, there are a considerable number of cosmetic changes to the cabinet and plate. I played a prototype of the new model at a trade show and found it to be one of the nicest sounding Young Chang pianos I've yet heard.

Young Chang has new "fashion model" vertical pianos with handsigned prints by Italian artists on the upper front panels. The prints can be ordered separately and fitted to any existing polyester-finish pianos. The price of this feature is about $800.

OTHER TOPICS

Chinese and Indonesian Pianos

1977 was the year that Chinese and Indonesian pianos joined the mainstream piano community. Several years of investment in infrastructure and training by piano manufacturers in joint venture with the Chinese government, and in Indonesia, have just started to bear fruit. Prior to this year, many pianos from this part of the world had too many obvious gross defects to be taken seriously. Most of the new manufacturing capacity in China is devoted to the market created by the rapidly growing Chinese middle class. A smaller portion is being diverted to the U.S. and other markets, aimed at consumers who would otherwise purchase an inexpensive used piano.

For some, these new Chinese and Indonesian pianos may indeed be a viable alternative to a used one, especially in areas where good used pianos are hard to come by or when shopping time is limited. But while many of these instruments are now acceptable, the quality is far from uniform or consistent, and the majority require extensive adjusting by the importer or dealer. Prospective customers should be reminded that these are, at best, entry-level pianos and that they have little or no track record. In addition, brand names and distributorships are in flux as the players position themselves in the market, so some warranties may offer less security than others. I would recommend, therefore, for the time being, that purchase be limited to those brands whose warranties are backed by major manufacturers or distributors. Additionally, a warranty from the dealer might be advisable.

Humidity Control

Dampp-Chaser Electronics Corp., which manufactures humidity-control equipment for pianos, has introduced several new models and enhancements, including systems that provide humidity control at the back of a vertical piano (where the design of the piano prevents placement of the system inside the front); systems that control humidity at both the back and front, for maximum protection; systems especially designed for climates that are unusually wet or unusually dry; and a "smart" heating element in the humidifier that turns itself off when no water is detected on the cloth pads.

MODEL and PRICING GUIDE

This guide contains the "list price" for nearly every brand, model, style, and finish of new piano that has regular distribution in the United States and, for the most part, Canada. Some marginal, local, or "stencil" brands are omitted. Except where indicated, prices are in U.S. dollars and the pianos are assumed to be for sale in the U.S. (Canadians will find the information useful after translation into Canadian dollars, but there may be differences in import duties and sales practices that will affect retail prices.) Prices and specifications are, of course, subject to change. Most manufacturers raise their prices at least once a year; two or three times a year is not uncommon when international currency values are unstable. The prices in this edition were compiled in the spring of 1997.

Some terms used in this guide require special explanation and disclaimers:

List Price

This is a "standard" list price computed according to a formula commonly used in the industry. The list price is usually a starting point for negotiation, not a final sales price. For their own suggested retail prices, some manufacturers use a different formula, usually one that raises the prices above "standard" list by ten to fifteen percent so that their dealers can advertise a larger "discount" without losing profit. For this reason, price-shopping by comparing discounts from the manufacturer's suggested retail price may result in a faulty price comparison. To provide a level playing field for comparing prices, most prices in this guide are computed according to the same "standard" formula, even though it may differ from the manufacturers' own suggested retail prices. [Exception: Some Steinway suggested retail prices are *lower* than "standard" list, but I'm using Steinway's prices in this guide because in many cases they are close to the actual selling prices, and comparison shopping is not as big an issue as it is with other brands.] For most models, the price includes a bench and the standard manufacturer's warranty for that brand (see *The Piano Book* for details). Most dealers will also include moving and one or two tunings in the home, but these are optional and a matter of agreement between you and the dealer.

Style and Finish

Unless otherwise indicated, the cabinet style is assumed to be "traditional" and is not stated. Exactly what "traditional" means varies from brand to brand. In general, it is a "classic" styling with minimal embellishment and straight legs. The vertical pianos have front legs, which are free-standing on smaller verticals and attached to the cabinet with toe blocks on larger verticals. "Continental" or European styling refers to vertical pianos without decorative trim and usually without front legs. Other furniture styles (Chippendale, French Provincial, Queen Anne, etc.) are as noted. The manufacturer's own trademarked style name is used when an appropriate generic name could not be determined.

Unless otherwise stated, all finishes are assumed to be "satin", which reflects light but not images. "Polished" finishes, also known as "high-gloss" or "high-polish", are mirror-like. "Oiled" finishes are usually matte (not shiny). "Open-pore" finishes, common on some European pianos, are slightly "grainier" satin finishes due to the wood pores not being filled in prior to finishing. "Ebony" is a black finish.

Special-order–only styles and finishes are in italics.

Some descriptions of style and finish may be slightly different from the manufacturer's own for the purpose of clarity, consistency, saving space, or other reason.

Size

The height of a vertical piano is measured from the floor to the top of the piano. The length of a grand piano is measured from the very front (keyboard end) to the very back (tail end).

About Actual Selling or "Street" Prices

Buying a piano is something like buying a car—the list price is deliberately set high in anticipation of negotiating.[*] But sometimes this is carried to extremes, as when the salesperson reduces the price three times in the first fifteen minutes to barely half the sticker price. In situations like this, the customer, understandably confused, is bound to ask in exasperation, "What is the *real* price of this piano?"

Unfortunately, there *is* no "real" price. In theory, the dealer pays a wholesale price and then marks it up by an amount sufficient to cover the overhead and produce a profit. In practice, however, the markup can vary considerably from sale to sale depending on such factors as:

---

[*] A relatively small number of dealers have non-negotiable prices.

- how long the inventory has been sitting around, racking up finance charges for the dealer

- how much of a discount the dealer received at the wholesale level for buying in quantity or for paying cash

- the dealer's cash flow situation

- the competition in that particular geographic area for a particular brand or type of piano

- special piano sales events taking place in the area

- how the salesperson sizes up your situation and your willingness to pay

- the level of pre- and post-sale service the dealer seeks to provide

- the dealer's other overhead expenses

It's not unusual for one person to pay fifty percent more than another for the same brand and model of piano—sometimes even from the same dealer on the same day! It may seem as if pricing is so chaotic that no advice can be given, but in truth, enough piano sales do fall within a certain range of typical profit margins that some guidance is possible as long as the reader understands the limitations inherent in this kind of endeavor.

Historically, discounts from "standard" list price have averaged ten or fifteen percent in the piano business. In recent years, however, conditions have changed such that, according to some industry sources, the average discount from list has increased to twenty or twenty-five percent. Essentially, due to growing competition from used pianos and digital pianos, and a decrease in the cultural importance attached to having a piano in the home, there are too many dealers of new pianos chasing after too few consumer dollars. In addition, higher labor costs worldwide and unfavorable international currency values make some brands so expensive in the U.S. that they can only be sold at very large discounts. I think, too, that consumers are becoming more savvy and are shopping around. Unfortunately, the overhead costs of running a traditional piano store are so high that most dealers cannot stay in business if they sell at an average discount from list price of more than about twenty percent. To survive, dealers are evolving multiple new approaches: becoming more efficient, instituting low-price/high volume strategies, cutting their overhead—sometimes including service—or subsidizing their meager sales of new pianos with used pianos (which command higher profit margins), rentals, rebuilding, and other products and services.

Although the average discount has increased, it is by no means uniform. Some brands dependably bring top dollar; others languish or the price is highly situational. I did consider giving a typical range of "street" prices for each brand and model listed in this volume, but concluded that the task would be too daunting due to the extreme variation that can exist from one situation to another, and because of the political fallout that would likely result from dealers and manufacturers who fear the loss of what little power they still have over aggressive, price-shopping customers. So, for now, I've decided just to give general advice in print. (For those who desire more specific information on "street" prices, I offer additional services, such as private telephone consultations and a Pricing Guide Service on the World Wide Web.)

It should be clearly understood that the advice given here is based on my own observations, subjective judgment, and general understanding of the piano market, *not* on statistical sales data or scientific analysis. (Brand-by-brand statistical sales data are virtually nonexistent.) This knowledge is the product of discussions with hundreds of customers, dealers, technicians, and industry executives over the years. Other industry observers may come to different conclusions. This rundown of "street" prices won't cover every brand, but should give a rough idea of what to expect and the ability to predict prices for some of the brands not specifically covered. I can't emphasize enough, however, that pricing can be highly situational, dependent on the mix of available products and the ease of comparison shopping in any particular geographic area, as well as on the financial situation of dealer and customer. The following generalizations should prove useful to you, but expect almost anything.

As a general rule of thumb:

- the more expensive the piano, the higher the possible discount

- the more "exclusive" a brand is perceived to be, the less likely head-to-head competition, and therefore the lower the possible discount

- the longer a piano remains unsold, the higher the possible discount

- the more service-intensive the piano, the lower the possible discount

Japanese and Korean brands are often perceived as being in direct competition with each other, as well as with those of the same national origin. Although discounts from "standard" list price on Japanese and Korean pianos typically start at perhaps fifteen percent, twenty or even thirty percent is not uncommon on the more expensive models or in a moderately competitive environment, especially if the dealer knows the customer is shopping around. Some Japanese and Korean companies tend to give large discounts at the wholesale level to dealers who buy in quantity, making it easy for those dealers to pass the savings on to the retail customer if they choose to do so.

Japanese pianos may be especially prone to deep discounting at times because they are less service-intensive than other brands (a testament to the perfection of their manufacturing processes) and because unfavorable currency values and higher labor costs make them relatively expensive. American-made pianos by Japanese companies are less expensive and probably less prone to deep discounting.

Korean pianos have the disadvantage of too many different brand names being made by the same two companies. When several of these are found in the same market, it tends to drive prices down. In addition, since Korean pianos are often the least expensive instruments in a dealer's inventory, the dealer may choose to sell one at a very low price to fit a very limited budget. Most dealers would rather sell you *something*, even at relatively little profit, than turn you away. For this reason, entry-level Korean grands in particular can be amazingly affordable.

The Boston piano, although manufactured in Japan, is generally viewed as being a little more exclusive due to its association with Steinway, so deep discounting is much less likely. The same principle holds true for Baldwin, whose pianos are usually seen as being distinctly different from the Asian products even though they often share common price ranges. Baldwin also benefits from exceptional name recognition and its historical "made in USA" connection. For both brands, discounting is likely to be moderate, in my experience.

Western European instruments tend to be extremely expensive here due to their high quality, the high European cost of doing business, and unfavorable exchange rates. There appear to be two types of dealers of these pianos. One type, usually specializing in selling higher-quality instruments to a demanding clientele, manages to get top dollar for them despite their high price, with discounts averaging only twenty percent or so. They are not particularly into negotiating. The other type of dealer, probably more numerous, depends for his or her "bread and butter" on consumer-grade pianos and is pleased to make a relatively small profit on the occasional sale of a luxury instrument. Discounts here may well approach forty percent at times, especially if the piano has gone unsold for an extended period of time.

At the other end of the price spectrum, most Russian and Chinese pianos are so cheap, and require so much servicing by the dealer, that it's simply not cost-effective to sell them for much less than full list price. Don't expect much in the way of discounts. Eastern European brands like Petrof are already seen as being a good deal for the money, have little in the way of direct competition, and are fairly service-intensive for the dealer, so expect lower than normal discounts off of list price.

Steinway pianos have always been in a class by themselves, historically the only expensive piano to continually command high profit margins. Except for older Steinways and the occasional Mason & Hamlin, Steinway has little competition and only about one hundred dealers in the United States. Service requirements can be quite high, at least in part because of the higher standards often required to satisfy a fussier clientele. Historically, Steinway pianos have sold at or near full manufacturer's suggested retail price. This is still true in many places, but in recent years I have seen a little more discounting than in the past. Ten to twenty percent is not unusual in some areas; as much as twenty-five percent would be rare.

There is no "fair" price for a piano except the one the buyer and seller agree on. The dealer is no more obligated to sell you a piano at a deep discount than you are obligated to pay the list price. Many dealers are simply not able to sell at the low end of the range consistently and still stay in business. It's understandable that you would like to pay the lowest price possible, and there's no harm in asking, but remember that piano shopping is not just about chasing the lowest price. Be sure you are getting the instrument that best suits your needs and preferences and that the dealer is committed to providing the proper pre- and post-sale service.

For more information on shopping for a new piano and on how to save money, please see pages 60–68 in *The Piano Book* (third edition).

Model	Size	Style and Finish	Price*

Astin-Weight

Verticals

375	41"	Ebony	6,700.
375	41"	Spanish Oiled Oak	6,950.
375	41"	Spanish Lacquer Oak	6,950.
375	41"	Italian Oiled Walnut	7,120.
375	41"	Italian Lacquer Walnut	7,160.
375	41"	Regency Oiled Oak	7,120.
375	41"	Regency Lacquer Oak	7,200.
375	41"	Regency Oiled Walnut	6,404.
375	41"	Regency Lacquer Walnut	7,240.
U-500	50"	Ebony	9,950.
U-500	50"	Oiled Oak	9,950.
U-500	50"	Lacquer Oak	10,070.
U-500	50"	Oiled Walnut	10,270.
U-500	50"	Lacquer Walnut	10,350.

Grands

———	5' 9"	Ebony	34,000.

August Förster — see "Förster, August"

Baldwin

Verticals

660	43-1/2"	Mahogany	4,180.
662	43-1/2"	Queen Anne Cherry	4,180.
665	43-1/2"	Country Oak	4,180.
667	43-1/2"	Country French Oak	4,180.
E100	43-1/2"	Continental Mahogany	4,100.
E100	43-1/2"	Continental Polished Ebony	4,700.
E100	43-1/2"	Continental Polished Ivory	4,700.
2090	43-1/2"	Hepplewhite Mahogany	4,900.
2095	43-1/2"	Oak	4,900.
2096	43-1/2"	Queen Anne Cherry	4,900.
243HPA	45"	Ebony	5,100.
243HPA	45"	Golden Oak	5,100.
243HPA	45"	American Walnut	5,100.

*For explanation of terms and prices, please see pages 29–34.

Model	Size	Style and Finish	Price*

Baldwin (continued)

Model	Size	Style and Finish	Price*
5050	45"	Limited Edition Mahogany	6,300.
5052	45"	Limited Edition Queen Anne Cherry	6,300.
5057	45"	Limited Edition Queen Anne Oak	6,300.
E250	45"	Contemporary Polished Ebony	5,300.
248A	48"	Ebony	6,900.
248A	48"	Polished Ebony	7,300.
248A	48"	American Walnut	7,100.
6000	52"	Ebony	8,900.
6000	52"	Mahogany	9,100.

Grands

Model	Size	Style and Finish	Price*
M	5' 2"	Ebony	20,220.
M	5' 2"	Polished Ebony	20,920.
M	5' 2"	Mahogany	21,120.
M	5' 2"	Polished Mahogany	21,820.
R	5' 8"	Ebony	22,900.
R	5' 8"	Polished Ebony	23,700.
R	5' 8"	Mahogany	23,900.
R	5' 8"	Polished Mahogany	24,700.
226	5' 8"	French Provincial Cherry	27,980.
226	5' 8"	French Provincial Polished Cherry	28,780.
227	5' 8"	Louis XVI Mahogany	27,740.
L	6' 3"	Ebony	25,560.
L	6' 3"	Polished Ebony	26,410.
L	6' 3"	Mahogany	26,660.
L	6' 3"	Polished Mahogany	27,510.
SF10	7'	Ebony	38,200.
SF10	7'	Polished Ebony	39,200.
SF10	7'	Mahogany	39,400.
SD10	9'	Ebony	61,400.

ConcertMaster (approximate, including installation by factory or dealer)

Verticals — Playback only		8,130.
Grands — Playback only		8,710.
Verticals — Playback w/Perf. Option		9,780.
Grands — Playback w/Perf. Option		10,360.

Note: Discounts may apply, especially as an incentive to purchase the piano.

Bechstein, C.

Verticals

Model	Size	Style and Finish	Price*
110	44"	Polished Ebony	21,030.
110	44"	Rufflelaquer Ebony	21,030.
110	44"	Mahogany	20,360.
110	44"	Oak	20,360.
110	44"	Walnut	21,030.
110	44"	Cherry	21,030.
110	44"	Polished White	21,820.
115	45"	Polished Ebony	24,980.
115	45"	Rufflelaquer Ebony	24,980.
115	45"	Mahogany	24,290.
115	45"	Oak	24,290.
115	45"	Walnut	24,980.
115	45"	Cherry	24,980.
115	45"	Polished White	25,750.
12N	45"	Polished Ebony	31,100.
12N	45"	Mahogany	30,100.
12N	45"	Oak	30,100.
12N	45"	Walnut	31,100.
12N	45"	Cherry	31,100.
12N	45"	Polished Woods (above)	32,080.
12N	45"	Polished White	32,080.
12N	45"	Yew	32,080.
12A	46"	Polished Ebony	33,540.
12A	46"	Mahogany	32,580.
12A	46"	Oak	32,580.
12A	46"	Walnut	33,540.
12A	46"	Cherry	33,540.
12A	46"	Polished Woods (above)	34,520.
12A	46"	Polished White	34,520.
12A	46"	Yew	34,520.
120	47"	Polished Ebony	27,100.
120	47"	Rufflelaquer Ebony	27,100.
120	47"	Mahogany	26,420.
120	47"	Oak	26,420.

*For explanation of terms and prices, please see pages 29–34.

Model	Size	Style and Finish	Price*
Bechstein, C. (continued)			
120	47"	Walnut	27,100.
120	47"	Cherry	27,100.
120	47"	Polished White	27,900.
122	48"	Polished Ebony	28,940.
122	48"	Cherry	28,940.
11A	48"	Polished Ebony	38,220.
11A	48"	Mahogany	37,240.
11A	48"	Oak	37,240.
11A	48"	Walnut	38,220.
11A	48"	Cherry	38,220.
11A	48"	Polished Woods (above)	39,200.
11A	48"	Polished White	39,200.
11A	48"	Yew	39,200.
8A	52"	Polished Ebony	42,200.
8A	52"	Mahogany	40,680.
8A	52"	Oak	40,680.
8A	52"	Walnut	42,200.
8A	52"	Cherry	42,200.
8A	52"	Polished Woods (above)	43,540.
8A	52"	Polished White	43,540.
8A	52"	Yew	43,540.
8A	52"	*Add for sostenuto*	2,380.
Grands			
K	5' 2"	Polished Ebony	75,360.
K	5' 2"	Mahogany	72,400.
K	5' 2"	Oak	72,400.
K	5' 2"	Walnut	75,360.
K	5' 2"	Cherry	75,360.
K	5' 2"	Polished Woods (above)	77,760.
K	5' 2"	Polished White	77,760.
K	5' 2"	Yew	77,760.
K	5' 2"	Chippendale Mahogany	78,880.
K	5' 2"	Chippendale Oak	78,880.
K	5' 2"	Chippendale Cherry	81,820.
K	5' 2"	Chippendale Walnut	81,820.
K	5' 2"	Chippendale Polished Woods (above)	83,780.

Model	Size	Style and Finish	Price*
M	5' 11"	Polished Ebony	82,860.
M	5' 11"	Mahogany	79,930.
M	5' 11"	Oak	79,930.
M	5' 11"	Walnut	82,860.
M	5' 11"	Cherry	82,860.
M	5' 11"	Polished Woods (above)	84,280.
M	5' 11"	Polished White	84,280.
M	5' 11"	Yew	84,280.
M	5' 11"	Chippendale Mahogany	85,480.
M	5' 11"	Chippendale Oak	85,480.
M	5' 11"	Chippendale Cherry	88,640.
M	5' 11"	Chippendale Walnut	88,640.
M	5' 11"	Chippendale Polished Woods (above)	90,080.
M	5' 11"	Classic Polished Ebony	90,080.
M	5' 11"	Classic Mahogany	87,120.
M	5' 11"	Classic Oak	87,120.
M	5' 11"	Classic Walnut	90,080.
M	5' 11"	Classic Cherry	90,080.
M	5' 11"	Classic Polished Woods (above)	93,680.
M	5' 11"	Classic Polished White	93,680.
M	5' 11"	Classic Yew	93,680.
189-A	6' 2"	Polished Ebony	67,780.
189-A	6' 2"	Rufflelaquer Ebony	67,780.
189-A	6' 2"	Mahogany	65,840.
189-A	6' 2"	Oak	65,840.
189-A	6' 2"	Walnut	67,780.
189-A	6' 2"	Cherry	67,780.
189-A	6' 2"	Polished White	70,240.
B	6' 10"	Polished Ebony	90,600.
B	6' 10"	Mahogany	89,200.
B	6' 10"	Oak	89,200.
B	6' 10"	Walnut	90,600.
B	6' 10"	Cherry	90,600.
B	6' 10"	Polished Woods (above)	93,500.
B	6' 10"	Polished White	93,500.
B	6' 10"	Yew	93,500.
B	6' 10"	Classic Polished Ebony	99,800.

*For explanation of terms and prices, please see pages 29–34.

Model	Size	Style and Finish	Price*

Bechstein, C. (continued)

Model	Size	Style and Finish	Price*
B	6' 10"	Classic Mahogany	98,400.
B	6' 10"	Classic Oak	98,400.
B	6' 10"	Classic Walnut	99,800.
B	6' 10"	Classic Cherry	99,800.
B	6' 10"	Classic Polished Woods (above)	102,680.
B	6' 10"	Classic Polished White	102,680.
B	6' 10"	Classic Yew	102,680.
C	7' 6"	Polished Ebony	108,940.
EN	9' 2"	Polished Ebony	135,240.

Becker, J.

Verticals

Model	Size	Style and Finish	Price*
BV-101	47"	Polished Ebony	2,498.
BV-101	47"	Mahogany	2,558.
BV-101	47"	Polished Mahogany	2,558.
BV-101	47"	Walnut	2,558.
BV-101	47"	Polished Walnut	2,558.
BV-101	47"	Polished Oak	2,598.
BV-101	47"	White	2,598.
BV-201	47"	Polished Ebony	2,698.
BV-201	47"	Mahogany	2,698.
BV-201	47"	Polished Mahogany	2,698.
BV-202	47"	Walnut	2,698.
BV-202	47"	Polished Walnut	2,698.
BV-301	47"	Polished Ebony	2,398.
BV-301	47"	Polished Mahogany	2,498.
BV-301	47"	Polished Walnut	2,498.
BV-301	47"	Polished Birchwood	2,538.

Grands

Model	Size	Style and Finish	Price*
BG-501	5' 2"	Polished Ebony	7,190.
BG-501	5' 2"	White	7,390.

Model	Size	Style and Finish	Price*

Blüthner

Verticals

Model	Size	Style and Finish	Price*
I	46"	Ebony	15,500.
I	46"	Polished Ebony	16,660.
I	46"	Walnut	16,860.
I	46"	Polished Walnut	18,320.
I	46"	Open-Pore Walnut	16,020.
I	46"	Mahogany	16,120.
I	46"	Polished Mahogany	17,340.
A	48"	Ebony	19,880.
A	48"	Polished Ebony	21,380.
A	48"	Walnut	21,640.
A	48"	Polished Walnut	23,520.
A	48"	Open-Pore Walnut	20,560.
A	48"	Mahogany	20,680.
A	48"	Polished Mahogany	22,220.
B	52"	Ebony	21,980.
B	52"	Polished Ebony	23,640.
B	52"	Walnut	23,920.
B	52"	Polished Walnut	26,000.
B	52"	Open-Pore Walnut	22,720.
B	52"	Mahogany	22,860.
B	52"	Polished Mahogany	24,540.

Grands

Model	Size	Style and Finish	Price*
11	5'	Ebony	39,400.
11	5'	Polished Ebony	42,380.
11	5'	Walnut	42,880.
11	5'	Polished Walnut	46,600.
11	5'	Open-Pore Walnut	40,740.
11	5'	Mahogany	40,980.
11	5'	Polished Mahogany	44,060.
11	5'	Polished Pyramid Mahogany	55,080.
11	5'	French Baroque Dark Walnut	57,200.
11	5'	French Baroque White	68,640.
10	5' 5"	Ebony	44,220.
10	5' 5"	Polished Ebony	47,560.

*For explanation of terms and prices, please see pages 29–34.

Model	Size	Style and Finish	Price*
Blüthner (continued)			
10	5' 5"	Walnut	48,120.
10	5' 5"	Polished Walnut	52,300.
10	5' 5"	Open-Pore Walnut	45,720.
10	5' 5"	Mahogany	45,980.
10	5' 5"	Polished Mahogany	49,460.
10	5' 5"	Polished Pyramid Mahogany	61,820.
10	5' 5"	French Baroque Dark Walnut	64,200.
10	5' 5"	French Barouqe White	77,040.
Haessler	6' 1"	Ebony	37,200.
Haessler	6' 1"	Polished Ebony	39,990.
Haessler	6' 1"	Walnut	40,400.
Haessler	6' 1"	Polished Walnut	44,000.
Haessler	6' 1"	Open-Pore Walnut	38,300.
Haessler	6' 1"	Mahogany	38,600.
Haessler	6' 1"	Polished Mahogany	41,500.
Haessler	6' 1"	Polished Pyramid Mahogany	51,800.
Haessler	6' 1"	French Baroque Dark Walnut	53,800.
Haessler	6' 1"	French Barouqe White	64,600.
Haessler	6' 1"	Classic Polished Ebony	45,900.
Haessler	6' 1"	Classic Polished Rosewood	47,700.
6	6' 2"	Ebony	49,680.
6	6' 2"	Polished Ebony	53,420.
6	6' 2"	Walnut	54,060.
6	6' 2"	Polished Walnut	58,760.
6	6' 2"	Open-Pore Walnut	51,360.
6	6' 2"	Mahogany	51,680.
6	6' 2"	Polished Mahogany	55,560.
6	6' 2"	Polished Pyramid Mahogany	69,440.
6	6' 2"	French Baroque Dark Walnut	72,120.
6	6' 2"	French Barouqe White	86,540.
6	6' 2"	Classic Polished Ebony	61,440.
6	6' 2"	Classic Polished Rosewood	63,900.
4	6' 10"	Ebony	55,880.
4	6' 10"	Polished Ebony	59,960.
4	6' 10"	Walnut	60,800.
4	6' 10"	Polished Walnut	66,080.

Model	Size	Style and Finish	Price*
4	6' 10"	Open-Pore Walnut	57,760.
4	6' 10"	Mahogany	58,100.
4	6' 10"	Polished Mahogany	62,480.
4	6' 10"	Polished Pyramid Mahogany	78,100.
4	6' 10"	Classic Polished Ebony	69,080.
4	6' 10"	Classic Polished Rosewood	71,860.
2	7' 6"	Ebony	62,700.
2	7' 6"	Polished Ebony	67,360.
2	7' 6"	*Mahogany*	
2	7' 6"	*Walnut*	
1	9' 2"	Ebony	73,200.
1	9' 2"	Polished Ebony	77,960.
1	9' 2"	*Mahogany*	
1	9' 2"	*Walnut*	

Bösendorfer

Verticals

130	52"	Polished Ebony	40,680.
130	52"	Walnut	43,980.
130	52"	Polished Walnut	43,980.
130	52"	Mahogany	43,980.
130	52"	Open-Pore Mahogany	43,980.
130	52"	Polished Mahogany	43,980.
130	52"	Polished White	43,980.
130	52"	Polished Rosewood	46,780.

Grands

170	5' 8"	Polished Ebony	79,180.
170	5' 8"	Walnut	83,580.
170	5' 8"	Polished Walnut	83,580.
170	5' 8"	Mahogany	83,580.
170	5' 8"	Open-Pore Mahogany	83,580.
170	5' 8"	Polished Mahogany	83,580.
170	5' 8"	Rosewood	88,980.
170	5' 8"	White	83,580.
170	5' 8"	Polished White	83,580.
170	5' 8"	Chippendale Mahogany	88,980.
170	5' 8"	Pyramid Mahogany	88,980.
170	5' 8"	Johann Strauss Polished Ebony	84,680.

*For explanation of terms and prices, please see pages 29–34.

Model	Size	Style and Finish	Price*
Bösendorfer (continued)			
200	6' 7"	Polished Ebony	92,380.
200	6' 7"	Walnut	100,380.
200	6' 7"	Open-Pore Walnut	100,380.
200	6' 7"	Polished Walnut	100,380.
200	6' 7"	Mahogany	100,380.
200	6' 7"	Open-Pore Mahogany	100,380.
200	6' 7"	Polished Mahogany	100,380.
200	6' 7"	Rosewood	105,180.
200	6' 7"	White	100,380.
200	6' 7"	Polished White	100,380.
200	6' 7"	Chippendale Mahogany	105,180.
200	6' 7"	Pyramid Mahogany	105,180.
200	6' 7"	Johann Strauss Polished Ebony	97,880.
200	6' 7"	Senator Polished Mahogany	107,180.
200	6' 7"	Franz Schubert Polished Cherry	105,180.
200	6' 7"	Millennium	128,580.
213	7'	Polished Ebony	105,580.
225	7' 4"	Polished Ebony	114,380.
225	7' 4"	Walnut	123,980.
225	7' 4"	Open-Pore Walnut	123,980.
225	7' 4"	Polished Walnut	123,980.
225	7' 4"	Mahogany	123,980.
225	7' 4"	Open-Pore Mahogany	123,980.
225	7' 4"	Polished Mahogany	123,980.
225	7' 4"	Pommele Mahogany	129,380.
225	7' 4"	Rosewood	129,380.
225	7' 4"	White	123,980.
225	7' 4"	Polished White	123,980.
225	7' 4"	Johann Strauss Polished Ebony	119,880.
225	7' 4"	Senator Polished Mahogany	131,380.
225	7' 4"	Franz Schubert Polished Cherry	129,380.
225	7' 4"	Millennium	157,580.
225	7' 4"	Polished H. Hollein	172,260.
275	9'	Polished Ebony	145,180.
290	9' 6"	Polished Ebony	175,980.

Model	Size	Style and Finish	Price*

Boston

Verticals

Model	Size	Style and Finish	Price*
UP-109C	43"	Continental Polished Ebony	6,190.
UP-109C	43"	Continental Polished White	6,590.
UP-118C	45"	Continental Polished Ebony	7,100.
UP-118C	45"	Continental Polished Walnut	7,740.
UP-118C	45"	Continental Polished Mahogany	7,740.
UP-118C	45"	Continental Polished White	7,530.
UP-118E	46"	Polished Ebony	7,530.
UP-118E	46"	Walnut	8,390.
UP-118E	46"	Polished Walnut	8,590.
UP-118E	46"	Polished Mahogany	8,590.
UP-118E	46"	Polished White	8,390.
UP-118S	46"	Open-Pore Honey Oak	5,390.
UP-118S	46"	Open-Pore Black Oak	5,390.
UP-118S	46"	Open-Pore Mahogany-Colored Oak	5,390.
UP-125E	49"	Polished Ebony	8,500.
UP-125E	49"	Polished Mahogany	9,790.
UP-132E	52"	Polished Ebony	10,300.

Grands

Model	Size	Style and Finish	Price*
GP-156	5' 1"	Ebony	13,980.
GP-156	5' 1"	Polished Ebony	13,980.
GP-163	5' 4"	Ebony	16,780.
GP-163	5' 4"	Polished Ebony	17,180.
GP-163	5' 4"	Mahogany	18,280.
GP-163	5' 4"	Polished Mahogany	18,720.
GP-163	5' 4"	Walnut	18,500.
GP-163	5' 4"	Polished Walnut	18,940.
GP-163	5' 4"	Polished White	17,640.
GP-163	5' 4"	Polished Ivory	17,640.
GP-178	5' 10"	Ebony	19,360.
GP-178	5' 10"	Polished Ebony	19,780.
GP-178	5' 10"	Mahogany	20,660.
GP-178	5' 10"	Polished Mahogany	21,080.
GP-178	5' 10"	Walnut	20,880.
GP-178	5' 10"	Polished Walnut	21,520.

*For explanation of terms and prices, please see pages 29–34.

Model	Size	Style and Finish	Price*

Boston (continued)

Model	Size	Style and Finish	Price*
GP-178	5' 10"	Polished White	20,220.
GP-178	5' 10"	Polished Ivory	20,220.
GP-193	6' 4"	Ebony	24,540.
GP-193	6' 4"	Polished Ebony	25,180.
GP-193	6' 4"	Walnut	27,340.
GP-193	6' 4"	Polished Mahogany	27,540.
GP-193	6' 4"	Polished White	26,480.
GP-218	7' 2"	Ebony	31,180.
GP-218	7' 2"	Polished Ebony	31,980.

Brentwood

Verticals

Model	Size	Style and Finish	Price*
MP005	42"	Continental Polished Ebony	2,590.
MP005	42"	Continental Polished Cherry	2,590.
MP005	42"	Continental Polished Dark Walnut	2,590.
MP005	42"	Continental Polished White	2,790.
CFR006	43"	Country French Polished Ebony	2,790.
CFR006	43"	Country French Walnut	2,790.
CFR006	43"	Country French Oak	2,790.
CFR006	43"	Country French Pecan	2,790.
CFR006	43"	Country French Mahogany	2,790.
CFR006	43"	Country French Polished White	3,070.
FR006	43"	French Cherry	2,830.
TR006	43"	Polished Ebony	2,790.
TR006	43"	Walnut	2,790.
TR006	43"	Oak	2,790.
TR006	43"	Pecan	2,790.
TR006	43"	Mahogany	2,790.
TR006	43"	Cherry	2,830.
TR006	43"	Polished White	2,990.
MP012	46"	Polished Ebony	2,990.
MP012	46"	Polished Cherry	2,990.
MP012	46"	Polished Dark Walnut	2,990.
MP012	46"	Polished White	3,090.

Charles R. Walter — see "Walter, Charles R."

Chickering

Grands

Model	Size	Style and Finish	Price
410A	4' 10"	Ebony	12,910.
410A	4' 10"	Polished Ebony	13,460.
410A	4' 10"	Mahogany	13,670.
410A	4' 10"	Polished Mahogany	14,260.
410QA	4' 10"	Queen Anne Cherry	14,580.
410QA	4' 10"	Queen Anne Polished Cherry	15,250.
507A	5' 7"	Ebony	15,120.
507A	5' 7"	Polished Ebony	15,710.
507A	5' 7"	Mahogany	16,070.
507A	5' 7"	Polished Mahogany	16,750.

Dobbert, Fritz

Verticals

Model	Size	Style and Finish	Price
108-04	42-1/2"	Continental Polished Mahogany	5,180.
108-07	42-1/2"	Continental Polished Imbuia	5,180.
108-11	42-1/2"	Continental Polished Ebony	5,180.
108-17	42-1/2"	Continental Imbuia	5,180.
109-04	43"	Polished Mahogany	5,580.
109-07	43"	Polished Imbuia	5,580.
109-11	43"	Polished Ebony	5,580.
109-17	43"	Imbuia	5,380.
113-14	43"	Mahogany	5,780.
116-11	45"	Polished Ebony	5,980.
126-04	50"	Polished Mahogany	7,380.
126-07	50"	Polished Imbuia	7,380.
126-11	50"	Polished Ebony	7,380.
126-17	50"	Imbuia	7,180.
127-04	50"	Polished Mahogany	7,380.
127-07	50"	Polished Imbuia	7,380.
127-11	50"	Polished Ebony	7,380.
127-17	50"	Imbuia	7,180.

*For explanation of terms and prices, please see pages 29–34.

Model	Size	Style and Finish	Price*

Estonia

Grands

Model	Size	Style and Finish	Price*
163	5' 4"	Ebony	14,800.
163	5' 4"	Polished Ebony	14,800.
163	5' 4"	White	14,800.
163	5' 4"	Polished White	14,800.
163	5' 4"	with Renner action, add	1,000.
190	6' 3"	Ebony	18,400.
190	6' 3"	Polished Ebony	18,400.
190	6' 3"	White	18,400.
190	6' 3"	Polished White	18,400.
190	6' 3"	*Chippendale Ebony*	19,800.
190	6' 3"	*Chippendale Polished Ebony*	19,800.
190	6' 3"	*Chippendale White*	19,400.
190	6' 3"	*Chippendale Polished White*	19,400.
190	6' 3"	with Renner action, add	1,000.
273	9'	Ebony	29,600.
273	9'	Polished Ebony	29,600.

Fandrich

Verticals

Model	Size	Style and Finish	Price*
Artist	48"	Ebony	14,800.

Fazioli

Fazioli is willing to make custom-designed cases with exotic veneers, marquetry, and other embellishments. Prices on request to Fazioli.

Grands

Model	Size	Style and Finish	Price*
F156	5' 2"	Ebony	65,400.
F156	5' 2"	Polished Ebony	66,800.
F156	5' 2"	Walnut	68,400.
F156	5' 2"	Polished Walnut	71,600.
F156	5' 2"	Polished Pyramid Mahogany	73,900.
F156	5' 2"	Cherry	68,400.
F156	5' 2"	Polished Cherry	71,600.

Model	Size	Style and Finish	Price*
F183	6'	Ebony	72,800.
F183	6'	Polished Ebony	74,400.
F183	6'	Walnut	76,400.
F183	6'	Polished Walnut	79,800.
F183	6'	Polished Pyramid Mahogany	82,700.
F183	6'	Cherry	76,400.
F183	6'	Polished Cherry	79,800
F212	6' 11"	Ebony	81,900.
F212	6' 11"	Polished Ebony	83,900.
F212	6' 11"	Walnut	85,900.
F212	6' 11"	Polished Walnut	89,900.
F212	6' 11"	Polished Pyramid Mahogany	93,000.
F212	6' 11"	Cherry	85,900.
F212	6' 11"	Polished Cherry	89,900.
F228	7' 6"	Ebony	91,900.
F228	7' 6"	Polished Ebony	93,900.
F228	7' 6"	Walnut	95,900.
F228	7' 6"	Polished Walnut	99,900.
F228	7' 6"	Polished Pyramid Mahogany	103,900.
F228	7' 6"	Cherry	95,900.
F228	7' 6"	Polished Cherry	99,900.
F278	9' 2"	Ebony	117,900.
F278	9' 2"	Polished Ebony	119,900.
F278	9' 2"	Walnut	123,200.
F278	9' 2"	Polished Walnut	128,700.
F278	9' 2"	Polished Pyramid Mahogany	133,200.
F278	9' 2"	Cherry	123,200.
F278	9' 2"	Polished Cherry	128,700.
F308	10' 2"	Ebony	155,500.
F308	10' 2"	Polished Ebony	157,900.
F308	10' 2"	Walnut	161,500.
F308	10' 2"	Polished Walnut	165,900.
F308	10' 2"	Polished Pyramid Mahogany	171,900.
F308	10' 2"	Cherry	161,500.
F308	10' 2"	Polished Cherry	165,900.

*For explanation of terms and prices, please see pages 29–34.

Model	Size	Style and Finish	Price*

Feurich

Grands

Model	Size	Style and Finish	Price*
F173	5' 10"	Polished Ebony	36,380.
F173	5' 10"	Polished Mahogany	37,180.
F173	5' 10"	*Polished Walnut*	37,180.
F173	5' 10"	*Polished White*	37,380.
F182	6'	Polished Ebony	37,380.
F182	6	Polished Mahogany	38,180.
F182	6'	*Polished Walnut*	38,180.
F182	6'	*Polished White*	38,380.
F208	6' 10"	Polished Ebony	42,780.
F208	6' 10"	Polished Mahogany	43,580.
F208	6' 10"	*Polished Walnut*	43,580.
F208	6' 10"	*Polished White*	43,780.

Förster, August

Verticals

Model	Size	Style and Finish	Price*
116C	46"	Chippendale Polished Ebony	17,800.
116C	46"	Chippendale Polished Walnut	17,800.
116E	46"	Polished Ebony	17,800.
116	46"	Polished White	18,800.
125G	50"	Polished Ebony	21,600.
125	50"	Polished White	22,600.

Grands

Model	Size	Style and Finish	Price*
170	5' 7"	Polished Ebony	37,000.
170	5' 7"	Polished Walnut	37,000.
170	5' 7"	Polished Mahogany	37,000.
170	5' 7"	Polished White	38,960.
170	5' 7"	Chippendale	45,000.
170	5' 7"	Antique	on request
170	5' 7"	Rococo	on request
190	6' 4"	Polished Ebony	42,000.
190	6' 4"	Polished Walnut	42,000.
190	6' 4"	Polished Mahogany	42,000.
190	6' 4"	Polished White	43,960.

Model	Size	Style and Finish	Price*
190	6' 4"	Chippendale	50,000.
190	6' 4"	Antique	on request
215	7' 2"	Polished Ebony	52,600.
275	9' 1"	Polished Ebony	106,000.

Fritz Dobbert — See "Dobbert, Fritz"

Grotrian

Grands

Model	Size	Style and Finish	Price*
165	5' 5"	Ebony	46,000.
165	5' 5"	Polished Ebony	49,000.
165	5' 5"	Polished Walnut	54,000.
165	5' 5"	Polished Mahogany	54,000.
192	6' 3"	Ebony	51,000.
192	6' 3"	Polished Ebony	56,000.
192	6' 3"	Polished Walnut	62,000.
192	6' 3"	Polished Mahogany	62,000.
225	7' 5"	Ebony	62,000.
225	7' 5"	Polished Ebony	67,000.
277	9' 2"	Polished Ebony	86,000.

Hoffmann, W.

Verticals

Model	Size	Style and Finish	Price*
H-115	45-1/2"	Polished Ebony	15,880.
H-115	45-1/2"	Oak	15,390.
H-115	45-1/2"	Mahogany	15,390.
H-115	45-1/2"	Polished Mahogany	16,860.
H-115	45-1/2"	Walnut	15,880.
H-115	45-1/2"	Polished Walnut	16,860.
H-115	45-1/2"	Cherry	15,880.
H-115	45-1/2"	Polished Cherry	16,860.
H-115	45-1/2"	Polished White	16,370.
H-115		Add for School Model (Satin Finishes)	770.
H-124	49"	Polished Ebony	17,580.
H-124	49"	Oak	16,920.
H-124	49"	Mahogany	16,920.

*For explanation of terms and prices, please see pages 29–34.

Model	Size	Style and Finish	Price*

Hoffmann, W. (continued)

Model	Size	Style and Finish	Price*
H-124	49"	Polished Mahogany	18,640.
H-124	49"	Walnut	17,580.
H-124	49"	Polished Walnut	18,640.
H-124	49"	Cherry	17,580.
H-124	49"	Polished Cherry	18,640.
H-124	49"	Polished White	18,280.
Grands			
H-180	6'	Polished Ebony	37,400.
H-180	6'	Polished Mahogany	40,100.

Hyundai

Verticals

Model	Size	Style and Finish	Price*
U-820	41"	Continental Ebony	3,898.
U-820	41"	Continental Polished Ebony	3,998.
U-820	41"	Continental Walnut	4,178.
U-820	41"	Continental Polished Walnut	4,178.
U-820	41"	Continental Polished Mahogany	4,178.
U-820	41"	Continental Polished Natural Oak	4,178.
U-820	41"	Continental Brown Oak	4,178.
U-820	41"	Continental Polished Brown Oak	4,178.
U-820	41"	Continental Polished Ivory	4,118.
U-820	41"	Continental Polished White	4,118.
U-824F	43"	French Walnut	4,998.
U-824F	43"	French Brown Oak	4,998.
U-824F	43"	French Cherry	4,998.
U-824M	43"	Mediterranean Brown Oak	4,998.
U-822	45"	Continental Polished Ebony	4,698.
U-822	45"	Continental Polished Mahogany	4,998.
U-852	46"	Ebony	5,198.
U-852	46"	Polished Ebony	5,198.
U-852	46"	Polished Mahogany	5,198.
U-852	46"	Brown Oak	5,198.
U-852	46"	Walnut	5,198.
U-842	46"	Chippendale Polished Mahogany	5,598.
U-832	48"	Ebony	5,198.

Model	Size	Style and Finish	Price*
U-832	48"	Polished Ebony	5,300.
U-832	48"	Walnut	5,398.
U-832	48"	Polished Walnut	5,398.
U-832	48"	Brown Oak	5,398.
U-832	48"	Polished Brown Oak	5,398.
U-832	48"	Polished Mahogany	5,398.
U-837	52"	Ebony	5,598.
U-837	52"	Polished Ebony	5,698.
U-837	52"	Walnut	5,798.
U-837	52"	Polished Walnut	5,798.
U-837	52"	Polished Mahogany	5,798.

Grands

Model	Size	Style and Finish	Price*
G-50A	4' 7"	Ebony	9,898.
G-50A	4' 7"	Polished Ebony	9,998.
G-50A	4' 7"	Walnut	10,398.
G-50A	4' 7"	Polished Walnut	10,398.
G-50A	4' 7"	Polished Mahogany	10,398.
G-50A	4' 7"	Brown Oak	10,398.
G-50A	4' 7"	Polished Brown Oak	10,398.
G-50A	4' 7"	Polished Natural Oak	10,398.
G-50A	4' 7"	Cherry	10,398.
G-50A	4' 7"	Polished Ivory	10,198.
G-50A	4' 7"	Polished White	10,198.
G-50A	4' 7"	Polished Rosewood	10,198.
G-50AF	4' 7"	Queen Anne Polished Ebony	11,900.
G-50AF	4' 7"	Queen Anne Walnut	11,900.
G-50AF	4' 7"	Queen Anne Polished Walnut	11,900.
G-50AF	4' 7"	Queen Anne Brown Oak	11,900.
G-50AF	4' 7"	Queen Anne Polished Brown Oak	11,900.
G-50AF	4' 7"	Queen Anne Polished Mahogany	11,900.
G-50AF	4' 7"	Queen Anne Cherry	11,900.
G-50AF	4' 7"	Queen Anne Polished Ivory	11,900.
G-50AF	4' 7"	Queen Anne Polished White	11,900.
G-80A	5' 1"	Ebony	11,398.
G-80A	5' 1"	Polished Ebony	11,498.
G-80A	5' 1"	Walnut	11,898.
G-80A	5' 1"	Polished Walnut	11,898.

*For explanation of terms and prices, please see pages 29–34.

Model	Size	Style and Finish	Price*
Hyundai (continued)			
G-80A	5' 1"	Polished Natural Oak	11,898.
G-80A	5' 1"	Brown Oak	11,898.
G-80A	5' 1"	Polished Brown Oak	11,898.
G-80A	5' 1"	Polished Mahogany	11,898.
G-80A	5' 1"	Cherry	11,898.
G-80A	5' 1"	Polished Ivory	11,698.
G-80A	5' 1"	Polished White	11,698.
G-80B	5' 1"	Chippendale Polished Mahogany	14,098.
G-80B	5' 1"	Chippendale Polished White	14,098.
G-81	5' 9"	Chippendale Polished Mahogany	15,398.
G-82	5' 9"	Ebony	12,798.
G-82	5' 9"	Polished Ebony	12,898.
G-82	5' 9"	Walnut	13,298.
G-82	5' 9"	Polished Walnut	13,298.
G-82	5' 9"	Polished Natural Oak	13,298.
G-82	5' 9"	Brown Oak	13,298.
G-82	5' 9"	Polished Brown Oak	13,298.
G-82	5' 9"	Polished Mahogany	13,298.
G-82	5' 9"	Cherry	13,298.
G-82	5' 9"	Polished Ivory	13,098.
G-82	5' 9"	Polished White	13,098.
G-82AF	5' 9"	Queen Anne Polished Mahogany	15,398.
G-82AF	5' 9"	Queen Anne Cherry	15,398.
G-84	6' 1"	Ebony	13,498.
G-84	6' 1"	Polished Ebony	13,598.
G-84	6' 1"	Walnut	13,998.
G-84	6' 1"	Polished Walnut	13,998.
G-84	6' 1"	Brown Oak	13,998.
G-84	6' 1"	Polished Brown Oak	13,998.
G-84	6' 1"	Polished Mahogany	13,998.
G-84	6' 1"	Polished Ivory	13,798.
G-84	6' 1"	Polished White	13,798.
G-85	6' 10"	Ebony	17,398.
G-85	6' 10"	Polished Ebony	17,398.

Ibach

Ibach pianos are distributed in Canada, but not in the U.S. Prices below are in Canadian dollars.

Verticals

Model	Size	Style and Finish	Price*
KI-115-S	46"	Polished Ebony	C9,359.
KI-115-S	46"	Polished Walnut	C9,717.
KI-115-S	46"	Polished Mahogany	C9,717.
KI-115-S	46"	*Cherry*	C9,895.
KI-115-S	46"	*Oak*	C9,895.
KI-115-S	46"	*White*	C9,895.
KI-115	46"	Polished Ebony	C10,252.
KI-115	46"	Polished Walnut	C10,612.
KI-115	46"	Polished Mahogany	C10,612.
KI-115	46"	*Cherry*	C10,790.
KI-115	46"	*Oak*	C10,790.
KI-115	46"	*White*	C10,790.
KI-122	48"	Polished Ebony	C10,973.
KI-122	48"	Polished Walnut	C11,334.
KI-122	48"	Polished Mahogany	C11,334.
KI-122	48"	*Cherry*	C11,505.
KI-122	48"	*Oak*	C11,505.
KI-122	48"	*White*	C11,505.
KI-126	50"	Polished Ebony	C11,334.
KI-126	50"	Polished Walnut	C11,685.
KI-126	50"	Polished Mahogany	C11,685.
KI-126	50"	*Cherry*	C11,866.
KI-126	50"	*Oak*	C11,866.
KI-126	50"	*White*	C11,866.

Grands

Model	Size	Style and Finish	Price*
KI-160	5' 3"	Polished Ebony	C22,589.
KI-160	5' 3"	*Polished Walnut*	C23,304.
KI-160	5' 3"	Polished Mahogany	C23,304.
KI-180	6'	Polished Ebony	C24,729.
KI-180	6'	*Polished Walnut*	C25,451.
KI-180	6'	Polished Mahogany	C25,451.
KI-215	7'	Polished Ebony	C32,956.

*For explanation of terms and prices, please see pages 29–34.

Model	Size	Style and Finish	Price*
Kawai			
Verticals			
CX-5	41"	Continental Polished Ebony	5,030.
CX-5	41"	Continental Polished Mahogany	5,150.
CX-5	41"	Continental Polished Walnut	5,150.
CX-5	41"	Continental Polished Ivory	5,070.
502-S	42"	Ebony	4,090.
502-S	42"	Oak	4,090.
503-M	42"	Mediterranean Oak	4,290.
503-T	42"	Mahogany	4,290.
503-F	42"	French Provincial Cherry	4,410.
503-Q	42"	Queen Anne Mahogany	4,410.
AT-503-M	42"	Mediterranean Oak with AnyTime	5,750.
AT-503-F	42"	French Provincial Cherry with AnyTime	5,870.
504-M	43"	Mediterranean Oak	3,990.
504-T	43"	Mahogany	3,990.
504-F	43"	French Provincial Cherry	4,090.
504-Q	43"	Queen Anne Mahogany	4,090.
604-M	44"	Mediterranean Pecan	5,290.
604-T	44"	Mahogany	5,370.
604-CF	44"	Country French Oak	5,410.
604-F	44"	French Provincial Cherry	5,410.
CE-11	44"	Continental Polished Ebony	6,770.
CE-11	44"	Continental Polished Sapeli Mahogany	7,370.
CX-5H	45"	Ebony	3,990.
CX-5H	45"	Polished Ebony	3,890.
CX-5H	45"	Oak	4,090.
CX-5H	45"	Polished Mahogany	4,590.
CX-5H	45"	Polished Snow White	4,090.
902-M	46"	Mediterranean Oak	6,070.
902-F	46"	French Provincial Cherry	6,290.
902-T	46"	Mahogany	6,290.
UST-7	46"	Ebony	6,070.
UST-7	46"	Oak	6,330.
UST-7	46"	Walnut	6,370.
UST-8C	46"	Ebony	5,050.

Model	Size	Style and Finish	Price*
UST-8C	46"	Walnut	5,050.
UST-8C	46"	Oak	5,050.
CX-21	48"	Polished Ebony	5,470.
CX-21	48"	Polished Snow White	5,470.
AT-120	48"	Polished Ebony with AnyTime	6,490.
NS-20A	49"	Polished Ebony	7,210.
NS-20A	49"	Oak	7,630.
NS-20A	49"	Walnut	7,850.
NS-20A	49"	Polished Walnut	8,330.
NS-20A	49"	Polished Sapeli Mahogany	8,190.
NS-20A LE	49"	Limited Edition Polished Ebony	7,410.
AT-170	49"	Polished Ebony with AnyTime	8,590.
US-6X	52"	Polished Ebony	9,590.
US-6X	52"	Polished Walnut	10,850.
US-8X	52"	Polished Ebony	11,750.
Grands			
GM-1	4' 9"	Ebony	11,690.
GM-1	4' 9"	Polished Ebony	11,790.
GM-1	4' 9"	Polished Snow White	12,790.
GM-2	5'	Ebony	11,090.
GM-2	5'	Polished Ebony	11,190.
GM-2	5'	Polished Snow White	11,990.
GE-1	5' 1"	Ebony	12,890.
GE-1	5' 1"	Polished Ebony	13,050.
GE-1	5' 1"	Walnut	14,590.
GE-1	5' 1"	Polished Mahogany	15,590.
GE-1	5' 1"	Polished Snow White	14,390.
GE-1	5' 1"	Polished Ivory	14,590.
GE-1A	5' 1"	Ebony	13,190.
GE-1A	5' 1"	Polished Ebony	13,390.
GE-1A	5' 1"	Polished Mahogany	15,790.
GE-1A	5' 1"	Polished Snow White	14,590.
GE-1A	5' 1"	Polished Ivory	14,990.
GE-1A LE	5' 1"	Limited Edition Polished Ebony	13,590.
RX-1	5' 5"	Ebony	16,690.
RX-1	5' 5"	Polished Ebony	16,990.
RX-1	5' 5"	Walnut	18,990.

*For explanation of terms and prices, please see pages 29–34.

Model	Size	Style and Finish	Price*

Kawai (continued)

Model	Size	Style and Finish	Price*
RX-1	5' 5"	Polished Walnut	19,790.
RX-1	5' 5"	Polished Sapeli Mahogany	19,590.
RX-1	5' 5'	Polished Snow White	18,790.
GE-3	5' 9"	Polished Ebony	17,390.
GE-3	5' 9"	Polished Snow White	18,790.
RX-2	5' 10"	Ebony	18,790.
RX-2	5' 10"	Polished Ebony	19,190.
RX-2	5' 10"	Walnut	20,790.
RX-2	5' 10"	Polished Walnut	21,590.
RX-2	5' 10"	Oak	19,790.
RX-2	5' 10"	Polished Sapeli Mahogany	21,190.
RX-2	5' 10"	Polished Mahogany	21,790.
RX-2	5' 10"	Polished Snow White	20,390.
RX-2	5' 10"	Polished Rosewood	25,090.
RX-2F	5' 10"	French Provincial Polished Mahogany	25,090.
RX-2 LE	5' 10"	Limited Edition Polished Ebony	19,590.
RX-3	6' 1"	Ebony	25,290.
RX-3	6' 1"	Polished Ebony	26,190.
RX-3 LE	6' 1"	Limited Edition Polished Ebony	26,590.
RX-A	6' 5"	Polished Ebony	51,990.
RX-5	6' 6"	Ebony	27,990.
RX-5	6' 6"	Polished Ebony	28,390.
RX-5	6' 6"	Limited Edition Polished Ebony	28,790.
RX-6	7'	Ebony	30,990.
RX-6	7'	Polished Ebony	31,390.
GS-100	9' 1"	Ebony	66,790.
GS-100	9' 1"	Polished Ebony	68,790.
EX	9' 1"	Polished Ebony	98,990.

Kemble

Verticals

Model	Size	Style and Finish	Price*
Cambridge 10	43"	Continental Polished Ebony	6,750.
Cambridge 10	43"	Continental Open-Pore Mahogany	5,995.
Cambridge 10	43"	Continental Polished Mahogany	6,750.
Cambridge 10	43"	*Continental Polished White*	6,995.

Model	Size	Style and Finish	Price*
Oxford	43"	Polished Ebony	6,995.
Oxford	43"	Open-Pore Mahogany	6,295.
Oxford	43"	Polished Mahogany	6,995.
Oxford	43"	Open-Pore Beech	6,995.
Cambridge 15	45"	Continental Polished Ebony	7,395.
Cambridge 15	45"	Continental Open-Pore Mahogany	6,750.
Cambridge 15	45"	Continental Open-Pore Cherry	6,995.
Traditional	45"	Polished Ebony	7,595.
Traditional	45"	Polished Mahogany	7,595.
Traditional	45"	Open-Pore Alder	7,395.
Prestige	45"	Open-Pore Cherry and Yew Inlay	8,550.
Empire	45"	Empire Polished Mahogany	8,750.
K121	48"	Polished Ebony	8,550.
K121	48"	Polished Mahogany	8,550.
Silent Verticals			
KS-15	45"	Cont. Open-Pore Walnut Color Mahog.	8,550.
KS Trad.	45"	Polished Ebony	9,195.
KS Empire	45"	Empire Polished Mahogany	10,550.

Knabe

The prices below include a factory-installed PianoDisc PDS 128 Plus or PianoCD playback system. Add $1,295 each for a Symphony Sound Module or a TFT MIDI Record System. Subtract $2,300 for a factory-installed GT-360 QuietTime system instead of the PDS 128 Plus or PianoCD. Subtract $3,500 for a regular Knabe acoustic piano without any extra equipment.

Verticals

Model	Size	Style and Finish	Price*
KN-420	42"	Continental Ebony	8,704.
KN-420	42"	Continental Polished Ebony	8,704.
KN-420	42"	Continental Polished Walnut	8,784.
KN-420	42"	Continental Polished Mahogany	8,784.
KN-420	42"	Continental Polished Ivory	8,704.
KN-420	42"	Continental Polished White	8,704.
KNF-43	43"	Queen Anne Oak	9,532.
KNF-43	43"	French Provincial Cherry	9,532.
KN-480	48"	Ebony	10,372.

*For explanation of terms and prices, please see pages 29–34.

Model	Size	Style and Finish	Price*
Knabe (continued)			
KN-480	48"	Polished Ebony	10,372.
KN-480	48"	Polished Walnut	10,666.
KN-480	48"	Polished Mahogany	10,666.
KN-480	48"	Polished Ivory	10,372.
KN-480	48"	Polished White	10,372.
KN-480NFI	48"	Open-Pore Walnut	10,754.
Grands			
KN-500	4' 11"	Ebony	17,086.
KN-500	4' 11"	Polished Ebony	17,086.
KN-500	4' 11"	Walnut	17,866.
KN-500	4' 11"	Polished Mahogany	17,866.
KN-500	4' 11"	Polished Ivory	17,086.
KN-500	4' 11"	Polished White	17,086.
KN-500QA	4' 11"	Queen Anne Mahogany	19,628.
KN-500QA	4' 11"	Queen Anne Polished Mahogany	19,628.
KN-520	5' 2"	Ebony	18,198.
KN-520	5' 2"	Polished Ebony	18,198.
KN-520	5' 2"	Walnut	18,764.
KN-520	5' 2"	Polished Mahogany	18,764.
KN-520	5' 2"	Polished Ivory	18,198.
KN-520	5' 2"	Polished White	18,198.
KN-520QA	5' 2"	Queen Anne Cherry	22,032.
KN-520QA	5' 2"	Queen Anne Mahogany	22,032.
KN-590	5' 9"	Ebony	20,240.
KN-590	5' 9"	Polished Ebony	20,240.
KN-590	5' 9"	Walnut	20,920.
KN-590	5' 9"	Polished Mahogany	20,920.
KN-590	5' 9"	Polished Ivory	20,240.
KN-590	5' 9"	Polished White	20,240.
KN-590EI	5' 9"	Empire Inlay Polished Mahogany	23,960.
KN-610	6' 1"	Ebony	20,692.
KN-610	6' 1"	Polished Ebony	20,692.
KN-610	6' 1"	Walnut	22,496.
KN-610	6' 1"	Polished Mahogany	22,496.
KN-610	6' 1"	Polished Ivory	20,692.

Model	Size	Style and Finish	Price*
KN-610	6' 1"	Polished White	20,692.
KN-700	6' 10"	Polished Ebony	26,620.

Kohler & Campbell

Verticals

Model	Size	Style and Finish	Price
SKV-108S	42"	Continental Ebony	3,980.
SKV-108S	42"	Continental Polished Ebony	3,980.
SKV-108S	42"	Continental Walnut	4,090.
SKV-108S	42"	Continental Polished Walnut	4,090.
SKV-108S	42"	Continental Polished Mahogany	4,090.
SKV-108S	42"	Continental Oak	4,090.
SKV-108S	42"	Continental Polished Oak	4,090.
SKV-108S	42"	Continental Polished Ivory	3,990.
SKV-108S	42"	Continental Polished White	3,990.
KC 043M	43"	Mediterranean Brown Oak	3,290.
KC 043F	43"	French Brown Oak	3,390.
KC 043F	43"	French Cherry	3,390.
KC 108	43"	Continental Polished Ebony	2,990.
KC 108	43"	Continental Walnut	2,790.
KC 108	43"	Continental Polished Walnut	3,090.
KC 108	43"	Continental Polished Mahogany	3,090.
KC 108	43"	Continental Polished Ivory	3,090.
KC 108	43"	Continental Polished White	3,090.
SKV-430FS	43"	French Provincial Cherry	3,790.
SKV-430FS	43"	French Provincial Oak	3,790.
SKV-430MS	43"	Mediterranean Oak	3,590.
SKV-430TS	43"	Cherry	4,090.
KC 112	44"	Polished Ebony	3,190.
KC 112	44"	Walnut	2,990.
KC 112	44"	Polished Walnut	3,290.
KC 112	44"	Polished Mahogany	3,290.
KC 112	44"	Polished Ivory	3,290.
KC 112	44"	Polished White	3,290.
SKV-465S	46-1/2"	Ebony	4,710.
SKV-465S	46-1/2"	Polished Ebony	4,710.
SKV-465S	46-1/2"	Walnut	4,930.

*For explanation of terms and prices, please see pages 29–34.

Model	Size	Style and Finish	Price*

Kohler & Campbell (continued)

Model	Size	Style and Finish	Price*
SKV-465S	46-1/2"	Polished Walnut	4,930.
SKV-465S	46-1/2"	Mahogany	4,930.
SKV-465S	46-1/2"	Polished Mahogany	4,930.
SKV-465S	46-1/2"	Oak	4,930.
SKV-465S	46-1/2"	Polished Oak	4,930.
SKV-470FS	46-1/2"	French Provincial Oak	4,790.
SKV-470FS	46-1/2"	French Provincial Cherry	4,790.
SKV-470MS	46-1/2"	Mediterranean Oak	4,590.
SKV-470TS	46-1/2"	Cherry	4,690.
SKV-48S	48"	Ebony	5,360.
SKV-48S	48"	Polished Ebony	5,360.
SKV-48S	48"	Walnut	5,530.
SKV-48S	48"	Polished Walnut	5,530.
SKV-48S	48"	Polished Mahogany	5,530.
SKV-48S	48"	Oak	5,530.
SKV-48S	48"	Polished Oak	5,530.
SKV-48S	48"	Polished Ivory	5,380.
SKV-48S	48"	Polished White	5,380.
SKV-52S	52"	Ebony	5,860.
SKV-52S	52"	Polished Ebony	5,860.
SKV-52S	52"	Walnut	5,960.
SKV-52S	52"	Polished Walnut	5,960.
SKV-52S	52"	Polished Mahogany	5,960.
SKV-52S	52"	Polished White	5,900.

Grands

Model	Size	Style and Finish	Price*
SKG-400S	4' 7"	Ebony	9,390.
SKG-400S	4' 7"	Polished Ebony	9,390.
SKG-400S	4' 7"	Walnut	9,790.
SKG-400S	4' 7"	Polished Walnut	9,790.
SKG-400S	4' 7"	Mahogany	9,790.
SKG-400S	4' 7"	Polished Mahogany	9,790.
SKG-400S	4' 7"	Oak	9,790.
SKG-400S	4' 7"	Polished Oak	9,790.
SKG-400S	4' 7"	Cherry	9,790.
SKG-400S	4' 7"	Polished Ivory	9,390.

Model	Size	Style and Finish	Price*
SKG-400S	4' 7"	Polished White	9,390.
SKG-400SCAF	4' 7"	French Provincial Walnut	11,810.
SKG-400SKBF	4' 7"	French Provincial Polished Walnut	11,810.
SKG-400SKBF	4' 7"	French Provincial Polished Mahogany	11,810.
SKG-400SKBF	4' 7"	French Provincial Polished Ivory	11,810.
SKG-500S	5' 1"	Ebony	10,990.
SKG-500S	5' 1"	Polished Ebony	10,990.
SKG-500S	5' 1"	Walnut	11,490.
SKG-500S	5' 1"	Polished Walnut	11,490.
SKG-500S	5' 1'	Mahogany	11,490.
SKG-500S	5' 1"	Polished Mahogany	11,490.
SKG-500S	5' 1"	Oak	11,490.
SKG-500S	5' 1"	Polished Oak	11,490.
SKG-500S	5' 1"	Cherry	11,490.
SKG-500S	5' 1"	Polished Ivory	10,990.
SKG-500S	5' 1"	Polished White	10,990.
SKG-500SKBF	5' 1"	French Provincial Polished Walnut	13,990.
SKG-500SKBF	5' 1"	French Provincial Polished Mahogany	13,990.
SKG-600S	5' 9"	Ebony	12,250.
SKG-600S	5' 9"	Polished Ebony	12,250.
SKG-600S	5' 9"	Walnut	12,550.
SKG-600S	5' 9"	Polished Walnut	12,550.
SKG-600S	5' 9"	Mahogany	12,550.
SKG-600S	5' 9"	Polished Mahogany	12,550.
SKG-600S	5' 9"	Oak	12,550.
SKG-600S	5' 9"	Polished Oak	12,550.
SKG-600S	5' 9"	Cherry	12,550.
SKG-600S	5' 9"	Polished Ivory	12,250.
SKG-600S	5' 9"	White	12,250.
SKG-600S	5' 9"	Polished White	12,250.
SKG-650S	6' 1"	Ebony	13,430.
SKG-650S	6' 1"	Polished Ebony	13,430.
SKG-650S	6' 1"	Walnut	13,730.
SKG-650S	6' 1"	Polished Walnut	13,730.
SKG-650S	6' 1"	Mahogany	13,730.
SKG-650S	6' 1"	Polished Mahogany	13,730.
SKG-650S	6' 1"	Oak	13,730.

*For explanation of terms and prices, please see pages 29–34.

Model	Size	Style and Finish	Price*

Kohler & Campbell (continued)

Model	Size	Style and Finish	Price*
SKG-650S	6' 1"	Polished Oak	13,730.
SKG-650S	6' 1"	Cherry	13,730.
SKG-700S	6' 10"	Ebony	17,590.
SKG-700S	6' 10"	Polished Ebony	17,590.
SKG-800S	7'	Ebony	20,660.
SKG-800S	7'	Polished Ebony	20,660.

Kranich & Bach

Verticals

Model	Size	Style and Finish	Price*
BP50	42"	Continental Polished Ebony	2,590.
BP50	42"	Continental Polished Cherry	2,590.

Maddison

Verticals

Model	Size	Style and Finish	Price*
108M	43"	Polished Ebony	2,890.
108M	43"	Polished Cherry	2,910.
108M2	43"	Chippendale Polished Ebony	2,920.
108M2	43"	Chippendale Polished Mahogany	2,970.
108M2	43"	Chippendale Polished Cherry	2,970.
108M2	43"	Chippendale Rosewood	2,970.
108M2	43"	Chippendale Polished White	2,990.
110R	44"	Fruitwood	3,450.
115M	45"	Polished Ebony	2,980.
115M	45"	Polished Cherry	3,050.
115M2	46"	Chippendale Polished Ebony	3,190.
115M2	46"	Chippendale Polished Cherry	3,240.
115M2	46"	Chippendale Polished Rosewood	3,240.
115M2	46"	Chippendale Polished White	3,290.

Grands

Model	Size	Style and Finish	Price*
GP-159	5' 3"	Polished Ebony	8,980.

Model	Size	Style and Finish	Price*

Maeari

Verticals

Model	Size	Style and Finish	Price*
MU820	41"	Continental Polished Ebony	3,998.
MU820	41"	Continental Polished Mahogany	4,178.
MU824T	43"	Brown Oak	4,798.
MU824F	43"	French Brown Oak	4,998.
MU824F	43"	French Cherry	4,998.
MU824M	43"	Mediterranean Brown Oak	4,998.
MU852	46"	Polished Ebony	5,198.
MU852	46"	Brown Oak	5,198.
MU842	46"	Chippendale Polished Mahogany	5,598.
MU832	48"	Polished Ebony	5,300.
MU832	48"	Walnut	5,398.
MU832	48"	Polished Walnut	5,398.
MU832	48"	Polished Mahogany	5,398.
MU837	52"	Polished Ebony	5,698.
MU837	52"	Polished Mahogany	5,798.

Grands

Model	Size	Style and Finish	Price*
G-450A	4' 7"	Ebony	9,898.
G-450A	4' 7"	Polished Ebony	9,998.
G-450A	4' 7"	Walnut	10,398.
G-450A	4' 7"	Polished Walnut	10,398.
G-450A	4' 7"	Polished Mahogany	10,398.
G-450A	4' 7"	Cherry	10,398.
G-450A	4' 7"	Polished Natural Oak	10,398.
G-450A	4' 7"	Brown Oak	10,398.
G-450A	4' 7"	Polished Brown Oak	10,398.
G-450A	4' 7"	Polished Ivory	10,198.
G-450A	4' 7"	Polished White	10,198.
G-450AF	4' 7"	Queen Anne Polished Ebony	11,900.
G-450AF	4' 7"	Queen Anne Walnut	11,900.
G-450AF	4' 7"	Queen Anne Polished Walnut	11,900.
G-450AF	4' 7"	Queen Anne Polished Mahogany	11,900.
G-450AF	4' 7"	Queen Anne Cherry	11,900.
G-450AF	4' 7"	Queen Anne Brown Oak	11,900.
G-450AF	4' 7"	Queen Anne Polished Brown Oak	11,900.

*For explanation of terms and prices, please see pages 29–34.

Model	Size	Style and Finish	Price*

Maeari (continued)

Model	Size	Style and Finish	Price*
G-450AF	4' 7"	Queen Anne Polished Ivory	11,900.
G-450AF	4' 7"	Queen Anne Polished White	11,900.
G-480A	5' 1"	Ebony	11,398.
G-480A	5' 1"	Polished Ebony	11,498.
G-480A	5' 1"	Walnut	11,898.
G-480A	5' 1"	Polished Walnut	11,898.
G-480A	5' 1"	Polished Mahogany	11,898.
G-480A	5' 1"	Cherry	11,898.
G-480A	5' 1"	Polished Natural Oak	11,898.
G-480A	5' 1"	Brown Oak	11,898.
G-480A	5' 1"	Polished Ivory	11,698.
G-480A	5' 1"	Polished White	11,698.
G-480B	5' 1"	Chippendale Polished Mahogany	14,098.
G-480AF	5' 1"	Queen Anne Polished Mahogany	14,098.
G-480AF	5' 1"	Queen Anne Cherry	14,098.
G-482	5' 9"	Ebony	12,798.
G-482	5' 9"	Polished Ebony	12,898.
G-482	5' 9"	Walnut	13,298.
G-482	5' 9"	Polished Walnut	13,298.
G-482	5' 9"	Polished Mahogany	13,298.
G-482	5' 9"	Polished Ivory	13,098.
G-482	5' 9"	Polished White	13,098.
G-481	5' 9"	Chippendale Polished Mahogany	15,398.
G-482AF	5' 9"	Queen Anne Polished Mahogany	15,398.
G-482AF	5' 9"	Queen Anne Cherry	15,398.
G-484	6' 1"	Polished Ebony	13,598.
G-484	6' 1"	Polished Mahogany	13,998.
G-484	6' 1"	Polished Ivory	13,798.
G-485	6' 10"	Ebony	17,398.
G-485	6' 10"	Polished Ebony	17,398.

Mason & Hamlin

Verticals

Model	Size	Style and Finish	Price*
50	50"	Ebony	13,390.
50	50"	Oak	13,590.

Model	Size	Style and Finish	Price*
50	50"	*Mahogany*	13,590.
50	50"	*Walnut*	13,590.
Grands			
A	5' 8"	Ebony	36,990.
A	5' 8"	Polished Ebony	37,990.
A	5' 8"	*Mahogany*	37,990.
A	5' 8"	*Polished Mahogany*	38,790.
A	5' 8"	*Walnut*	39,590.
A	5' 8"	*Polished Walnut*	40,390.
BB	7'	Ebony	46,990.
BB	7'	Polished Ebony	47,990.
BB	7'	*Mahogany*	47,990.
BB	7'	*Polished Mahogany*	48,590.
BB	7'	*Walnut*	51,190.
BB	7'	*Polished Walnut*	51,990.

Nakamura (formerly Nakamichi)

Model	Size	Style and Finish	Price*
Verticals			
N-121	48"	Polished Ebony	5,990.
N-121	48"	Polished Mahogany	6,790.
N-131	52"	Polished Ebony	6,990.
N-131	52"	Polished Mahogany	7,790.
Grands			
N-157	5' 2"	Polished Ebony	13,990.
N-157	5' 2"	Polished Mahogany	14,990.
N-185	6' 1"	Polished Ebony	15,590.
N-185	6' 1"	Polished Mahogany	16,590.

Niemeyer

Model	Size	Style and Finish	Price*
Verticals			
NI112	44"	Continental Polished Ebony	2,700.
NI112	44"	Continental Polished Mahogany	2,700.
NI112	44"	Continental Polished Walnut	2,700.
NI112	44"	Continental Polished White	2,790.
NI114	45"	Polished Ebony	2,900.

*For explanation of terms and prices, please see pages 29–34.

Model	Size	Style and Finish	Price*

Niemeyer (continued)

Model	Size	Style and Finish	Price*
NI114	45"	Polished Mahogany	2,900.
NI121	48"	Polished Ebony	3,100.
NI121	48"	Polished Mahogany	3,100.

Pearl River

Verticals

Model	Size	Style and Finish	Price*
UP-108A	43"	Continental Polished Ebony	2,950.
UP-108A	43"	Continental Polished Walnut	2,950.
UP-108A	43"	Continental Pol. Burgundy Mahogany	2,950.
UP-108A	43"	Continental Polished Cherry Mahogany	2,950.
UP-108B	43"	Continental Polished Ebony	2,870.
UP-108B	43"	Continental Polished Walnut	2,870.
UP-108B	43"	Continental Pol. Burgundy Mahogany	2,870.
UP-108B	43"	Continental Polished Cherry Mahogany	2,870.
UP-108B	43"	Continental Polished White	2,870.
UP-108M	43"	Polished Ebony	2,870.
UP-108M	43"	Polished Walnut	2,870.
UP-108M	43"	Polished Burgundy Mahogany	2,870.
UP-108M	43"	Polished Cherry Mahogany	2,870.
UP-108M	43"	Fruitwood	2,870.
UP-108M-2	43"	Chippendale Polished Ebony	2,950.
UP-108M-2	43"	Chippendale Polished Walnut	2,950.
UP-108M-2	43"	Chippendale Pol. Burgundy Mahogany	2,950.
UP-108M-2	43"	Chippendale Polished Cherry Mahogany	2,950.
UP-110P-2	43"	Chippendale Walnut	3,470.
UP-110P-2	43"	Chippendale Mahogany	3,470.
UP-110R	43"	Walnut	3,470.
UP-110R	43"	Mahogany	3,470.
UP-110R	43"	Fruitwood	3,470.
UP-114B	45"	Continental Polished Ebony	2,990.
UP-114B	45"	Continental Polished Walnut	2,990.
UP-114B	45"	Continental Pol. Burgundy Mahogany	2,990.
UP-114B	45"	Continental Polished Cherry Mahogany	2,990.
UP-114B	45"	Continental Polished White	2,990.
UP-115M	45"	Polished Ebony	2,990.

Model	Size	Style and Finish	Price*
UP-115M	45"	Polished Walnut	2,990.
UP-115M	45"	Polished Burgundy Mahogany	2,990.
UP-115M	45"	Polished Cherry Mahogany	2,990.
UP-118M	46"	Polished Ebony	3,150.
UP-118M	46"	Polished Walnut	3,150.
UP-118M	46"	Polished Burgundy Mahogany	3,150.
UP-118M	46"	Polished Cherry Mahogany	3,150.
UP-118M-2	46"	Chippendale Polished Ebony	3,390.
UP-118M-2	46"	Chippendale Polished Walnut	3,390.
UP-118M-2	46"	Chippendale Pol. Burgundy Mahogany	3,390.
UP-118M-2	46"	Chippendale Polished Cherry Mahogany	3,390.
UP-121M	48"	Polished Ebony	3,750.
UP-121M	48"	Polished White	3,750.
UP-130M	51"	Polished Ebony	3,670.
UP-130M	51"	Polished Walnut	3,670.
UP-130M	51"	Polished Burgundy Mahogany	3,670.
UP-130M-1	51"	Chippendale Polished Ebony	3,990.
UP-130M-1	51"	Chippendale Polished Walnut	3,990.
UP-130M-1	51"	Chippendale Pol. Burgundy Mahogany	3,990.
UP-130M-1	51"	Chippendale Polished Cherry Mahogany	3,990.
UP-130T	51"	Deluxe Polished Ebony	4,650.
Grands			
GP-159	5' 2-1/2"	Polished Ebony	8,990.
GP-159	5' 2-1/2"	Polished Walnut	9,190.
GP-159	5' 2-1/2"	Polished Burgundy Mahogany	9,190.
GP-159	5' 2-1/2"	Polished White	9,190.
GP-213	7'	Polished Ebony	17,800.
GP-213	7'	Polished White	17,800.
GP-275	9'	Polished Ebony *(available Fall 1997)*	

Petrof

Note: Prices below do not include bench. Add from $220 to $630 (most are under $400), depending on choice of bench.

Verticals

Model	Size	Style and Finish	Price*
100-B	42"	Barok Polished Walnut	6,100.
100-B	42"	Barok Polished Flame Mahogany	6,100.
100-S	42"	Continental Polished Ebony	4,980.

*For explanation of terms and prices, please see pages 29–34.

Model	Size	Style and Finish	Price*

Petrof (continued)

Model	Size	Style and Finish	Price*
100-S	42"	Continental Polished Walnut	4,980.
100-S	42"	Continental Polished Flame Mahogany	4,980.
105-I	42"	Antique Polished Ebony	5,580.
105-I	42"	Antique Polished Walnut	5,580.
105-I	42"	Antique Polished Flame Mahogany	5,580.
115-I	45"	Demi-Chippendale Polished Ebony	5,700.
115-I	45"	Demi-Chippendale Polished Walnut	5,700.
115-I	45"	Demi-Chippendale Pol. Flame Mahog.	5,700.
115-I	45"	Rococo White with Gold Trim	6,500.
115-IC	45"	Chippendale Polished Ebony	5,980.
115-IC	45"	Chippendale Polished Walnut	5,980.
115-IC	45"	Chippendale Polished Flame Mahogany	5,980.
115-II	45"	Continental Polished Ebony	5,180.
115-II	45"	Continental Polished Walnut	5,180.
115-II	45"	Continental Polished Flame Mahogany	5,180.
115-II	45"	Continental Polished Oak	5,180.
115-IID	45"	Polished Ebony	5,700.
115-IID	45"	Polished Walnut	5,700.
115-IID	45"	Polished Flame Mahogany	5,700.
115-VI	45"	Polished Ebony	5,500.
115-VI	45"	Polished Walnut	5,500.
115-VI	45"	Polished Flame Mahogany	5,500.
125-II	50"	Polished Ebony	6,580.
125-II	50"	Polished Walnut	6,580.
125-II	50"	Polished Flame Mahogany	6,580.
126	50"	Polished Ebony with Walnut trim	6,980.
131	52"	Polished Ebony	9,380.
131	52"	Polished Walnut	9,380.
131	52"	Polished Flame Mahogany	9,380.

Grands

Model	Size	Style and Finish	Price*
V	5' 3"	Polished Ebony	17,180.
V	5' 3"	Polished Walnut	17,180.
V	5' 3"	Polished Flame Mahogany	17,180.
IV	5' 8"	Polished Ebony	18,380.
IV	5' 8"	Polished Walnut	18,380.

Model	Size	Style and Finish	Price*
IV	5' 8"	Polished Flame Mahogany	18,380.
IV C	5' 8"	Chippendale Polished Ebony	23,180.
IV C	5' 8"	Chippendale Polished Walnut	23,180.
IV C	5' 8"	Chippendale Polished Flame Mahogany	23,180.
III	6' 4"	Polished Ebony	21,980.
III	6' 4"	Polished Walnut	21,980.
III	6' 4"	Polished Flame Mahogany	21,980.
III M	6' 4"	Polished Ebony	30,780.
II	7' 9"	Polished Ebony	33,580.
I	9' 3"	Polished Ebony	42,780.

PianoDisc

Note: "PianoDisc" pianos have been discontinued. See under "Knabe".

Prices for PianoDisc and QuietTime systems vary by piano manufacturer and installer. The following are suggested retail prices from Music Systems Research. The usual dealer discounts may apply, especially as an incentive to purchase a piano.

PDS 128 Plus System, "factory-installed" or retrofitted:

Playback only	5,195.
Add for Symphony Sound Module	1,295.
Add for TFT MIDI Record option	1,295.
Add for amplified speakers, pair	599.

PianoCD System (playback with CD accompaniment) 4,500.

QuietTime System: GT-360 2,699.

GT-90 1,999.

MIDI Controller (TFT MIDI Strip and MIDI interface board) 1,799.

QRS / Pianomation

Prices for Pianomation systems vary by piano manufacturer and installer. The following are suggested retail prices from QRS. The usual dealer discounts may apply, especially as an incentive to purchase a piano.

Pianomation: "Piano Solo" (CD-ROM *or* 3.5" floppy) 4,700.

Add for Orchestration option 500.

*For explanation of terms and prices, please see pages 29–34.

Model	Size	Style and Finish	Price*

QRS / Pianomation (continued)

		Add for Record option	900.
		Less for customer-supplied CD player	300.
		Add for both CD-ROM *and* 3.5" floppy	450.
Playola:		Playola with Orchestration, speakers, amplifier, and carrying case	6,200.

Ridgewood

Verticals

Model	Size	Style and Finish	Price
110	43"	French Cherry	3,550.
110	43"	Italian Walnut	3,550.
110	43"	Mahogany	3,550.

Grands

159	5' 2"	Polished Ebony	8,990.
159	5' 2"	Polished Mahogany	9,190.
159	5' 2"	Polished Walnut	9,190.
159	5' 2"	Polished White	9,190.

Rieger-Kloss

Verticals

Model	Size	Style and Finish	Price
R-109	43"	Continental Polished Ebony	5,300.
R-109	43"	Continental Walnut	5,300.
R-109	43"	Continental Polished Walnut	5,300.
R-109	43"	Continental Polished Mahogany	5,300.
R-109	43"	Continental Light Oak	5,300.
R-111	44"	Rustic Oak	4,700.
R-111	44"	Light Beech	4,700.
R-111	44"	Light Walnut	4,700.
R-118	47"	Contemporary Polished Ebony	5,580.
R-118	47"	Contemporary Walnut	5,580.
R-118	47"	Contemporary Cherry	5,580.
R-118	47"	Contemporary Light Oak	5,580.
R-121	48"	Polished Ebony	6,050.
R-122	48"	Demi-Chippendale Polished Ebony	6,710.
R-122	48"	Demi-Chippendale Polished Walnut	6,710.

Model	Size	Style and Finish	Price*
R-122	48"	Demi-Chippendale Mahogany	6,710.
R-123	48"	Polished Ebony	6,510.
R-123	48"	Polished Walnut	6,510.
R-123	48"	Polished Mahogany	6,510.
R-125	50"	Polished Ebony	8,990.
R-126	50"	Polished Ebony	7,190.
R-126	50"	Polished Mahogany	7,190.
Grands			
R-185	6' 1"	Polished Ebony	21,970.

Sagenhaft

Verticals

Model	Size	Style and Finish	Price*
S-111	44-1/2"	Continental Polished Ebony	2,800.
S-111	44-1/2"	Continental Polished Walnut	2,900.
S-111	44-1/2"	Continental Polished Mahogany	2,900.
S-115L	44-1/2"	Polished Ebony	3,200.
S-115L	44-1/2"	Polished Walnut	3,300.
S-115L	44-1/2"	Polished Mahogany	3,300.
S-116C	45-1/2"	Continental Polished Ebony	3,700.
S-116C	45-1/2"	Continental Polished Walnut	3,800.
S-116C	45-1/2"	Continental Polished Mahogany	3,800.
S-116S	45-1/2"	Chippendale Polished Ebony	3,800.
S-116S	45-1/2"	Chippendale Polished Walnut	3,900.
S-116S	45-1/2"	Chippendale Polished Mahogany	3,900.
S-116CA	45-1/2"	Baroque Polished Ebony	4,240.
S-116CA	45-1/2"	Baroque Polished Walnut	4,340.
S-116CA	45-1/2"	Baroque Polished Mahogany	4,340.
S-121L	48"	Polished Ebony	3,720.
S-121L	48"	Polished Walnut	3,820.
S-126L	50"	Polished Ebony	4,200.
S-126L	50"	Polished Walnut	4,300.
Grands			
159	5' 2"	Polished Ebony	8,990.
159	5' 2"	Polished Mahogany	9,190.
159	5' 2"	Polished Walnut	9,190.
159	5' 2"	Polished White	9,190.

*For explanation of terms and prices, please see pages 29–34.

Samick

Verticals

Model	Size	Style and Finish	Price*
SU-108P	42"	Continental Polished Ebony	3,980.
SU-108P	42"	Continental Walnut	4,090.
SU-108P	42"	Continental Polished Walnut	4,090.
SU-108P	42"	Continental Polished Mahogany	4,090.
SU-108P	42"	Continental Oak	4,090.
SU-108P	42"	Continental Polished Oak	4,090.
SU-108P	42"	Continental Polished Ivory	3,980.
SU-108P	42"	Continental Polished White	3,980.
JS 043M	43"	Mediterranean Brown Oak	3,290.
JS 043F	43"	French Brown Oak	3,390.
JS 043F	43"	French Cherry	3,390.
JS 108	43"	Continental Polished Ebony	2,990.
JS 108	43"	Continental Walnut	2,790.
JS 108	43"	Continental Polished Walnut	3,090.
JS 108	43"	Continental Polished Mahogany	3,090.
JS 108	43"	Continental Polished Ivory	3,090.
JS 108	43"	Continental Polished White	3,090.
SU-143F	43"	French Provincial Cherry	3,790.
SU-143F	43"	French Provincial Oak	3,790.
SU-143M	43"	Mediterranean Oak	3,590.
SU-143MR	43"	Mediterranean Oak	4,090.
SU-143T	43"	Cherry	3,690.
JS 112	44"	Polished Ebony	3,190.
JS 112	44"	Walnut	2,990.
JS 112	44"	Polished Walnut	3,290.
JS 112	44"	Polished Mahogany	3,290.
JS 112	44"	Polished Ivory	3,290.
JS 112	44"	Polished White	3,290.
SU-118FA	46-1/2"	Continental Polished Walnut	5,750.
SU-118FA	46-1/2"	Continental Polished Mahogany	5,750.
SU-118H	46-1/2"	Continental Polished Ebony	4,590.
SU-118H	46-1/2"	Continental Walnut	4,790.
SU-118H	46-1/2"	Continental Polished Walnut	4,790.
SU-118H	46-1/2"	Continental Mahogany	4,790.

Model	Size	Style and Finish	Price*
SU-118H	46-1/2"	Continental Polished Mahogany	4,790.
SU-118H	46-1/2"	Continental Oak	4,790.
SU-118H	46-1/2"	Continental Polished Oak	4,790.
SU-118H	46-1/2"	Continental Polished Ivory	4,590.
SU-118H	46-1/2"	Continental Polished White	4,590.
SU-147S	46-1/2"	Ebony	4,610.
SU-147S	46-1/2"	Polished Ebony	4,610.
SU-147S	46-1/2"	Walnut	4,830.
SU-147S	46-1/2"	Polished Walnut	4,830.
SU-147S	46-1/2"	Mahogany	4,830.
SU-147S	46-1/2"	Polished Mahogany	4,830.
SU-147S	46-1/2"	Oak	4,830.
SU-147S	46-1/2"	Polished Oak	4,830.
SU-347F	46-1/2"	French Provincial Oak	4,690.
SU-347F	46-1/2"	French Provincial Cherry	4,690.
SU-347M	46-1/2"	Mediterranean Oak	4,490.
SU-347T	46-1/2"	Cherry	4,590.
SU-121B	48"	Ebony	5,260.
SU-121B	48"	Polished Ebony	5,260.
SU-121B	48"	Walnut	5,430.
SU-121B	48"	Polished Walnut	5,430.
SU-121B	48"	Mahogany	5,430.
SU-121B	48"	Polished Mahogany	5,430.
SU-131B	52"	Ebony	5,760.
SU-131B	52"	Polished Ebony	5,760.
SU-131B	52"	Walnut	5,860.
SU-131B	52"	Polished Walnut	5,860.
SU-131B	52"	Mahogany	5,860.
SU-131B	52"	Polished Mahogany	5,860.

Grands

Model	Size	Style and Finish	Price*
SG-150	4' 11-1/2"	Ebony	9,600.
SG-150	4' 11-1/2"	Polished Ebony	9,600.
SG-150	4' 11-1/2"	Walnut	10,100.
SG-150	4' 11-1/2"	Polished Walnut	10,100.
SG-150	4' 11-1/2"	Mahogany	10,100.
SG-150	4' 11-1/2"	Polished Mahogany	10,100.
SG-150	4' 11-1/2"	Oak	10,100.

*For explanation of terms and prices, please see pages 29–34.

Model	Size	Style and Finish	Price*
Samick (continued)			
SG-150	4' 11-1/2"	Polished Oak	10,100.
SG-150	4' 11-1/2"	Cherry	10,100.
SG-150	4' 11-1/2"	Polished Ivory	9,700.
SG-150	4' 11-1/2"	Polished White	9,700.
SG-150KA/BF	4' 11-1/2"	French Provincial Ebony	11,960.
SG-150KA/BF	4' 11-1/2"	French Provincial Polished Ebony	11,960.
SG-150KA/BF	4' 11-1/2"	French Provincial Walnut	11,960.
SG-150KA/BF	4' 11-1/2"	French Provincial Polished Walnut	11,960.
SG-150KA/BF	4' 11-1/2"	French Provincial Mahogany	11,960.
SG-150KA/BF	4' 11-1/2"	French Provincial Polished Mahogany	11,960.
SG-150KA/BF	4' 11-1/2"	French Provincial Oak	11,960.
SG-150KA/BF	4' 11-1/2"	French Provincial Polished Oak	11,960.
SG-150KA/BF	4' 11-1/2"	French Provincial Cherry	11,960.
SG-150KA/BF	4' 11-1/2"	French Provincial Polished Ivory	11,960.
SG-150KA/BF	4' 11-1/2"	French Provincial Polished White	11,960.
SG-161	5' 3-1/2"	Ebony	11,080.
SG-161	5' 3-1/2"	Polished Ebony	11,080.
SG-161	5' 3-1/2"	Walnut	11,590.
SG-161	5' 3-1/2"	Polished Walnut	11,590.
SG-161	5' 3-1/2"	Mahogany	11,590.
SG-161	5' 3-1/2"	Polished Mahogany	11,590.
SG-161	5' 3-1/2"	Oak	11,590.
SG-161	5' 3-1/2"	Polished Oak	11,590.
SG-161	5' 3-1/2"	Cherry	11,590.
SG-161	5' 3-1/2"	Polished Ivory	11,100.
SG-161	5' 3-1/2"	Polished White	11,100.
SG-172	5' 7"	Ebony	12,050.
SG-172	5' 7"	Polished Ebony	12,050.
SG-172	5' 7"	Walnut	12,350.
SG-172	5' 7"	Polished Walnut	12,350.
SG-172	5' 7"	Mahogany	12,350.
SG-172	5' 7"	Polished Mahogany	12,350.
SG-172	5' 7"	Oak	12,350.
SG-172	5' 7"	Polished Oak	12,350.
SG-172	5' 7"	Cherry	12,350.
SG-172	5' 7"	Polished Ivory	12,100.

Model	Size	Style and Finish	Price*
SG-172	5' 7"	Polished White	12,100.
SG-185	6' 1"	Ebony	13,230.
SG-185	6' 1"	Polished Ebony	13,230.
SG-185	6' 1"	*Walnut*	13,530.
SG-185	6' 1"	*Polished Walnut*	13,530.
SG-185	6' 1"	*Mahogany*	13,530.
SG-185	6' 1"	*Polished Mahogany*	13,530.
SG-185	6' 1"	*Oak*	13,530.
SG-185	6' 1"	*Polished Oak*	13,530.
SG-185	6' 1"	*Polished Ivory*	13,530.
SG-185	6' 1"	*Polished White*	13,530.
WSG-185	6' 1"	Ebony	18,700.
WSG-185	6' 1"	Polished Ebony	18,700.
WSG-185	6' 1"	*All other finishes (see above)*	19,100.
WSG-205	6' 8"	Ebony	21,640.
WSG-205	6' 8"	Polished Ebony	21,640.
WSG-205	6' 8"	*All other finishes (see above)*	22,040.
WSG-225	7' 4"	Ebony	27,200.
WSG-225	7' 4"	Polished Ebony	27,200.
WSG-225	7' 4"	*All other finishes (see above)*	27,600.
WSG-275	9' 1"	Ebony	49,990.
WSG-275	9' 1"	Polished Ebony	49,990.
WSG-275	9' 1"	*All other finishes (see above)*	51,990.

Sängler & Söhne / Wieler

Verticals

Model	Size	Style and Finish	Price*
USC-110	44"	Continental Polished Ebony	2,070.
USC-110	44"	Continental Mahogany	1,990.
USC-110	44"	Continental Polished Mahogany	2,050.
USC-110	44"	Continental Polished White	2,130.
BE-110K	45"	Polished Ebony	2,390.
BE-110K	45"	Polished Mahogany	2,370.
BE-110K	45"	Polished White	2,450.
USC-120	48"	Polished Ebony	2,590.
USC-120	48"	Polished Mahogany	2,570.
USC-120	48"	Polished White	2,650.
USC-120	48"	French Polished Mahogany	2,590.

*For explanation of terms and prices, please see pages 29–34.

Model	Size	Style and Finish	Price*

Sauter

These pianos are purchased by the dealer directly from Sauter in Germany. Prices will depend on the cost of freight, duty, and other charges. The prices below are FOB Germany and do not include a bench.

Verticals

Model	Size	Style and Finish	Price
112-C	44"	"Carus" Ebony	11,058.
112-C	44"	"Carus" Polished Ebony	11,058.
112-N	44"	"Nova" Ebony	12,394.
112-N	44"	"Nova" Polished Ebony	13,576.
112-N	44"	"Nova" Mahogany	12,394.
112-N	44"	"Nova" Walnut	12,394.
112-N	44"	"Nova" Oak	12,394.
112-N	44"	"Nova" Cherry	13,024.
112-N	44"	"Nova" Polished White	13,808.
112-S	44"	"Schulpiano" Oak	11,816.
112-S	44"	"Schulpiano" Walnut	11,816.
114-A	45"	"Andiamo" Polished Ebony	13,178.
114-A	45"	"Andiamo" Mahogany	13,640.
114-A	45"	"Andiamo" Oak	13,640.
114-A	45"	"Andiamo" Walnut	13,640.
114-A	45"	"Andiamo" Cherry	12,870.
114-A	45"	"Andiamo" Yew	13,178.
114-A	45"	"Andiamo" Beech	12,472.
114-A	45"	"Andiamo" Polished White	13,486.
114-R	45"	"Ragazza" Polished Ebony	13,486.
114-R	45"	"Ragazza" Walnut	13,268.
114-R	45"	"Ragazza" Polished White	13,250.
120-N	47"	"Nova" Walnut	14,284.
120-N	47"	"Nova" Oak	14,284.
120-P	47"	"Premiere" Ebony	13,884.
120-P	47"	"Premiere" Polished Ebony	14,836.
120-P	47"	"Premiere" Mahogany	13,884.
120-P	47"	"Premiere" Polished Mahogany	15,722.
120-P	47"	"Premiere" Walnut	13,884.
120-P	47"	"Premiere" Oak	13,884.
120-P	47"	"Premiere" Cherry	14,284.

Model	Size	Style and Finish	Price*
120-P	47"	"Premiere" Yew	14,772.
120-P	47"	"Premiere" Polished White	15,324.
122-AV	48"	"Avenue" Oak	15,800.
122-C	48"	"Carat" Polished Ebony	19,320.
122-D	48"	"Domino" Polished Ebony	15,144.
122-D	48"	"Domino" Pear	14,976.
122-D	48"	"Domino" Beech	14,604.
122-D	48"	"Domino" Maple	14,682.
122-M1	48"	"M-Line 1" Polished Ebony	21,234.
122-M2	48"	"M-Line 2" Polished Ebony	18,330.
122-PM	48"	"Peter Maly" Polished Ebony	21,760.
122-PM	48"	"Peter Maly" Cherry	19,204.
122-PM	48"	"Peter Maly" Custom Finish	18,792.
122-R	48"	"Resonance" Ebony	15,864.
122-R	48"	"Resonance" Polished Ebony	16,442.
122-R	48"	"Resonance" Walnut	15,722.
122-R	48"	"Resonance" Oak	15,722.
122-R	48"	"Resonance" Cherry	16,044.
122-R	48"	"Resonance" Pine	15,722.
122-R	48"	"Resonance" Yew	16,364.
122-S	48"	"Schulpiano" Oak	12,678.
122-S	48"	"Schulpiano" Walnut	12,678.
122-TL	48"	"True-Love" Walnut	15,080.
122-TL	48"	"True-Love" Yew	17,456.
122-TL	48"	"True-Love" Polished Yew	18,254.
130-C	51"	"Competence" Polished Ebony	18,254.
130-C	51"	"Competence" Walnut	17,316.
130-C	51"	"Competence" Polished White	18,574.

Grands

Model	Size	Style and Finish	Price*
160-A	5' 3"	"Alpha" Ebony	31,192.
160-A	5' 3"	"Alpha" Polished Ebony	35,496.
160-A	5' 3"	"Alpha" Polished White	35,020.
160-C	5' 3"	Chippendale Mahogany	33,312.
160-C	5' 3"	Chippendale Walnut	33,312.
160-N	5' 3"	"Noblesse" Walnut	35,920.
160-N	5' 3"	"Noblesse" Polished Walnut	40,416.
160-N	5' 3"	"Noblesse" Cherry	36,922.

*For explanation of terms and prices, please see pages 29–34.

Model	Size	Style and Finish	Price*

Sauter (continued)

Model	Size	Style and Finish	Price*
185-C	6' 1"	Chippendale Mahogany	35,998.
185-C	6' 1"	Chippendale Walnut	35,998.
185-D	6' 1"	"Delta" Polished Ebony	38,592.
185-D	6' 1"	"Delta" Walnut	34,700.
185-D	6' 1"	"Delta" Polished White	39,466.
185-N	6' 1"	"Noblesse" Walnut	38,618.
185-N	6' 1"	"Noblesse" Polished Walnut	43,244.
185-N	6' 1"	"Noblesse" Cherry	39,684.
185-PM	6' 1"	"Peter Maly" Custom Finish	50,452.
220-O	7' 3"	"Omega" Polished Ebony	49,154.

Schimmel

Verticals

Model	Size	Style and Finish	Price*
112 E	45"	Empire Polished Mahogany	12,580.
112 S	45"	Open-pore Walnut	12,580.
112 S	45"	Open-pore Oak	11,980.
114 K	45"	Classicism Polished Ebony	12,280.
114 K	45"	Classicism Polished White	12,680.
116 S	46"	Special Polished Ebony	10,980.
120 I	48"	International Polished Ebony	12,280.
120 J	48"	Centennial Polished Mahogany	13,080.
120 LE	48"	*Lyra Exquisite Polished Ebony*	12,880.
120 LE	48"	Lyra Exquisite Polished Mahogany	13,080.
120 RI	48"	Royale Intarsia Polished Mahogany	14,980.
120 T	48"	Polished Ebony	12,680.
120 T	48"	*Polished Walnut*	12,880.
120 T	48"	*Polished Mahogany*	12,880.
120 T	48"	Polished White	13,080.
120 TN	48"	Noblesse Polished Ebony	12,880.
120 TN	48"	Noblesse Polished White	13,280.
122 KE	49"	Classicism Exquisite Polished Ebony	12,880.
122 KE	49"	Classicism Exquisite Polished Mahogany	13,080.
130 T	51"	Polished Ebony	14,780.
130 T	51"	*Polished Walnut*	14,980.
130 T	51"	Polished Mahogany	14,980.

Model	Size	Style and Finish	Price*

Grands

When not mentioned, satin finish available on special order at same price as high-polish finish.

Model	Size	Style and Finish	Price*
SP 174 T	5' 10"	Ebony	31,980.
SP 174 T	5' 10"	Polished Ebony	31,980.
SP 174 T	5' 10"	*Polished Walnut*	32,780.
SP 174 T	5' 10"	Polished Mahogany	32,780.
SP 174 T	5' 10"	*Polished White*	32,980.
SP 174 C	5' 10"	*Chippendale Polished Ebony*	34,980.
SP 174 C	5' 10"	*Chippendale Polished Walnut*	35,780.
SP 174 C	5' 10"	*Chippendale Polished Mahogany*	35,780.
SP 174 C	5' 10"	*Chippendale Polished White*	35,980.
SP 174 E	5' 10"	*Empire Polished Mahogany*	40,380.
SP 174 LE	5' 10"	Limited Edition Polished Ebony	34,980.
SP 174 S	5' 10"	Oak	31,180.
SP 174 TE	5' 10"	Exquisite Polished Ebony	33,580.
SP 174 TE	5' 10"	Exquisite Polished Mahogany	34,380.
SP 174 TE	5' 10"	*Exquisite Polished White*	34,580.
SP 174 TEI	5' 10"	Exquisite Intarsia Mahogany	35,580.
SP 174 TJ	5' 10"	Jubilee Polished Ebony	33,980.
SG 174 TJ	5' 10"	*Jubilee Polished Cherry*	34,580.
SG 174 TJ	5' 10"	Jubilee Polished Mahogany	34,980.
SP 182 T	6'	Ebony	32,980.
SP 182 T	6'	Polished Ebony	32,980.
SP 182 T	6'	*Polished Walnut*	33,780.
SP 182 T	6'	Polished Mahogany	33,780.
SP 182 T	6'	*Polished White*	33,980.
SP 182 C	6'	*Chippendale Polished Ebony*	35,980.
SP 182 C	6'	*Chippendale Polished Walnut*	36,780.
SP 182 C	6'	*Chippendale Polished Mahogany*	36,780.
SP 182 C	6'	*Chippendale Polished White*	36,980.
SP 182 E	6'	*Empire Polished Mahogany*	41,380.
SP 182 LE	6'	Limited Edition Polished Ebony	35,980.
SP 182 S	6'	Oak	32,180.
SP 182 TE	6'	Exquisite Polished Ebony	34,580.
SP 182 TE	6'	Exquisite Polished Mahogany	35,380.
SP 182 TE	6'	*Exquisite Polished White*	35,580.

*For explanation of terms and prices, please see pages 29–34.

Model	Size	Style and Finish	Price*

Schimmel (continued)

Model	Size	Style and Finish	Price*
SP 182 TEI	6'	Exquisite Intarsia Mahogany	36,580.
SG 182 TJ	6'	Jubilee Polished Ebony	34,980.
SG 182 TJ	6'	*Jubilee Polished Cherry*	35,580.
SG 182 TJ	6'	Jubilee Polished Mahogany	35,980.
CC 208 T	6' 10"	Polished Ebony	37,780.
CC 208 T	6' 10"	*Polished Walnut*	38,580.
CC 208 T	6' 10"	*Polished Mahogany*	38,580.
CC 208 T	6' 10"	*Polished White*	38,780.
CC 208 LE	6' 10"	Polished Ebony	41,180.
CC 208 S	6' 10"	Oak	36,580.
CC 208 G	6' 10"	*Plexiglass*	81,400.
CC 208 P	6' 10"	*Pegasus Polished Ebony*	153,800.
CO 256 C	8' 4"	Polished Ebony	59,800.

Schirmer & Son

Verticals

Model	Size	Style and Finish	Price*
M-105C	42"	Continental Polished Ebony	4,590.
M-105C	42"	Continental Polished Mahogany	4,590.
M-113CH	44"	Queen Anne Polished Mahogany	5,990.
M-113CH	44"	Queen Anne Polished Walnut	5,990.
M-118A	47"	Polished Ebony	5,990.
M-118A	47"	Polished Mahogany	5,990.
M-118A	47"	Polished Walnut	5,990.
M-118A	47"	Oak	5,990.
M-118CH	47"	Chippendale Polished Ebony	6,190.
M-118CH	47"	Chippendale Polished Mahogany	6,190.
M-118CH	47"	Chippendale Polished Walnut	6,190.
M-118CH	47"	Chippendale Polished White	6,590.
M-128E	51"	Polished Ebony	6,790.
M-128E	51"	Polished Mahogany	6,790.
M-128E	51"	Polished Walnut	6,790.

Grands

Model	Size	Style and Finish	Price*
M-163	5' 4"	Polished Ebony	14,990.
M-190	6' 3"	Polished Ebony	17,990.
M-273	9'	Polished Ebony	37,990.

Model	Size	Style and Finish	Price*

Schubert

Verticals

Model	Size	Style and Finish	Price*
B-16	43"	Continental Polished Ebony	2,190.
B-16	43"	Continental Polished Mahogany	2,190.
B-16	43"	Continental Polished Oak	2,190.
B-17	44"	Oak	2,190.
B-17	44"	Mahogany	2,190.
B-17	44"	French Provincial Oak	2,390.
B-17	44"	French Provincial Mahogany	2,390.
B-18	44"	Polished Ebony	2,250.
B-18	44"	Polished Mahogany	2,250.
B-18	44"	Polished Oak	2,250.
B-15	47"	Polished Ebony	2,290.
B-15	47"	Polished Mahogany	2,290.
B-15	47"	Polished Oak	2,290.

Seiler

Verticals

Model	Size	Style and Finish	Price*
116	46"	Favorit Open-Pore Ebony	12,726.
116	46"	Favorit Polished Ebony	13,738.
116	46"	Favorit Open-Pore Walnut	12,726.
116	46"	Favorit Open-Pore Oak	12,726.
116	46"	Favorit Polished White	14,062.
116	46"	School Open-Pore Ebony	12,726.
116	46"	School Open-Pore Oak	12,726.
116	46"	Mondial Open-Pore Ebony	13,076.
116	46"	Mondial Open-Pore Walnut	13,076.
116	46"	Mondial Open-Pore Mahogany	13,076.
116	46"	Mondial Polished Mahogany	13,738.
116	46"	Mondial Open-Pore Oak	13,076.
116	46"	Mondial Open-Pore Cherry	13,738.
116	46"	Jubilee Polished Ebony	14,038.
116	46"	Jubilee Polished White	14,250.
116	46"	Chippendale Open-Pore Walnut	13,212.
116	46"	Escorial Open-Pore Cherry Intarsia	14,250.

*For explanation of terms and prices, please see pages 29–34.

Model	Size	Style and Finish	Price*
Seiler (continued)			
122	48"	Konsole Open-Pore Ebony	13,438.
122	48"	Konsole Polished Ebony	14,376.
122	48"	Konsole Open-Pore Walnut	13,438.
122	48"	Konsole Open-Pore Oak	13,438.
122	48'	Konsole Open-Pore Cherry	14,126.
122	48"	Konsole Polished White	14,750.
122	48"	School Open-Pore Ebony	12,838.
122	48"	School Open-Pore Walnut	12,838.
122	48"	School Open-Pore Oak	12,838.
122	48"	Vienna Polished Ebony	14,938.
122	48"	Vienna Polished Mahogany with Inlays	16,650.
122	48"	Vienna Polished Walnut with Inlays	16,650.
122	48"	Vienna Open-Pore Cherry Intarsia	15,538.
122	48"	Designer Polished Ebony	15,738.
122	48"	Designer Open-Pore Cherry/Macassar	15,738.
131	52"	Concert SMR Polished Ebony	15,750.
131	52"	Concert SMR Open-Pore Walnut	14,800.
131	52"	Concert Polished Mahogany	16,238.
Grands			
180	5' 11"	Polished Ebony	34,526.
180	5' 11"	Open-Pore Walnut	32,812.
180	5' 11"	Polished Walnut	35,838.
180	5' 11"	Open-Pore Mahogany	32,812.
180	5' 11"	Polished Mahogany	35,838.
180	5' 11"	Polished White	35,312.
180	5' 11"	Chippendale Open-Pore Walnut	35,426.
180	5' 11"	Westminster Polished Mahogany Intarsia	46,726.
180	5' 11"	Florenz Polished Walnut/Myrtle Intarsia	46,726.
180	5' 11"	Florenz Polished Mahogany/Myrtle Intar	46,726.
180	5' 11"	Louvre Polished Ebony	37,412.
180	5' 11"	Louvre Polished Cherry Intarsia	46,726.
180	5' 11"	Louvre Polished White	38,050.
180	5' 11"	Showmaster Chrome/Brass/Polyester	93,950.
206	6' 9"	Polished Ebony	38,726.
240	8'	Polished Ebony	53,738.

Model	Size	Style and Finish	Price*

Steigerman

Verticals

Model	Size	Style and Finish	Price*
ST-109A	43"	Continental Polished Ebony	3,150.
ST-109A	43"	Continental Polished Mahogany	3,290.
ST-109A	43"	Continental Polished Walnut	3,290.
ST-109B	43"	Continental Polished Ebony	3,200.
ST-109B	43"	Continental Polished Mahogany	3,340.
ST-109B	43"	Continental Polished Walnut	3,340.
ST-109C	43"	Continental Polished Ebony	3,230.
ST-109C	43"	Continental Polished Mahogany	3,370.
ST-109C	43"	Continental Polished Walnut	3,370.
ST-115	45"	Polished Ebony	3,380.
ST-115	45"	Polished Mahogany	3,540.
ST-115	45"	Polished Walnut	3,540.
ST-115C	45"	Polished Ebony	3,400.
ST-115C	45"	Polished Mahogany	3,560.
ST-115C	45"	Polished Walnut	3,560.
ST-122	48"	Polished Ebony	4,200.
ST-122	48"	Polished Mahogany	4,360.
ST-122	48"	Polished Walnut	4,360.
ST-122C	48"	Polished Ebony	4,230.
ST-122C	48"	Polished Mahogany	4,390.
ST-122C	48"	Polished Walnut	4,390.

Grands

Model	Size	Style and Finish	Price*
ST-168XS	5' 6"	Polished Ebony	9,000.

Steinway & Sons

† *denotes Crown Jewel Collection and Limited Edition models*

Verticals

Model	Size	Style and Finish	Price*
4510	45"	Sheraton Ebony	14,300.
4510	45"	Sheraton Mahogany	15,100.
4510	45"	Sheraton Walnut	15,700.
4510	45"	*Add for high-polish finish*	2,700.
4510	45"	†140th Anniv. Hepplewhite Mahogany	15,900.
1098	46-1/2"	Ebony	13,200.
1098	46-1/2"	Mahogany	13,800.

*For explanation of terms and prices, please see pages 29–34.

Model	Size	Style and Finish	Price*

Steinway & Sons (continued)

Model	Size	Style and Finish	Price*
1098	46-1/2"	Walnut	14,400.
1098	46-1/2"	*Add for high-polish finish*	2,700.
K-52	52"	Ebony	17,300.
K-52	52"	Mahogany	18,700.
K-52	52"	Walnut	19,300.
K-52	52"	*Add for high-polish finish*	3,600.

Grands

Model	Size	Style and Finish	Price*
S	5' 1"	Ebony	29,100.
S	5' 1"	Mahogany	31,900.
S	5' 1"	Walnut	33,100.
S	5' 1"	*Add for high-polish finish*	3,900.
S	5' 1"	†Figured Sapele	35,700.
S	5' 1"	†Kewazinga Bubinga	37,100.
S	5' 1"	†East Indian Rosewood	41,700.
S	5' 1"	†Santos Rosewood	41,100.
S	5' 1"	†Macassar Ebony	45,900.
S	5' 1"	†Hepplewhite Dark Cherry	37,800.
M	5' 7"	Ebony	33,600.
M	5' 7"	Mahogany	36,500.
M	5' 7"	Walnut	37,700.
M	5' 7"	*Add for high-polish finish*	4,500.
M	5' 7"	†Figured Sapele	40,100.
M	5' 7"	†Kewazinga Bubinga	42,100.
M	5' 7"	†East Indian Rosewood	46,900.
M	5' 7"	†Santos Rosewood	46,300.
M	5' 7"	†Macassar Ebony	51,800.
M	5' 7"	†Hepplewhite Dark Cherry	43,100.
M SK-1014	5' 7"	Chippendale Mahogany	45,800.
M SK-1014	5' 7"	Chippendale Walnut	47,100.
M SK-501	5' 7"	Louis XV Walnut	59,900.
M	5' 7"	†Louis XV Rosewood	71,100.
L	5' 10-1/2"	Ebony	37,900.
L	5' 10-1/2"	Mahogany	41,100.
L	5' 10-1/2"	Walnut	42,400.
L	5' 10-1/2"	*Add for high-polish finish*	5,100.

Model	Size	Style and Finish	Price*
L	5' 10-1/2"	†Figured Sapele	45,200.
L	5' 10-1/2"	†Kewazinga Bubinga	47,300.
L	5' 10-1/2"	†East Indian Rosewood	52,700.
L	5' 10-1/2"	†Santos Rosewood	52,100.
L	5' 10-1/2"	†Macassar Ebony	58,800.
L	5' 10-1/2"	†Hepplewhite Dark Cherry	48,500.
L SK-390	5' 10-1/2"	†J. B. Tiffany East Indian Rosewood	78,800.
L SK-390	5' 10-1/2"	†J. B. Tiffany African Pommele	79,200.
B	6' 10-1/2"	Ebony	49,200.
B	6' 10-1/2"	Mahogany	52,900.
B	6' 10-1/2"	Walnut	54,400.
B	6' 10-1/2"	*Add for high-polish finish*	6,500.
B	6' 10-1/2"	†Figured Sapele	58,100.
B	6' 10-1/2"	†Kewazinga Bubinga	60,800.
B	6' 10-1/2"	†East Indian Rosewood	67,200.
B	6' 10-1/2"	†Santos Rosewood	66,500.
B	6' 10-1/2"	†Macassar Ebony	74,900.
B	6' 10-1/2"	†Hepplewhite Dark Cherry	62,300.
B SK-390	6' 10-1/2"	†J. B. Tiffany East Indian Rosewood	96,200.
B SK-390	6' 10-1/2"	†J. B. Tiffany African Pommele	97,600.
D	8' 11-3/4"	Ebony	74,800.
D	8' 11-3/4"	Mahogany	81,600.
D	8' 11-3/4"	Walnut	83,300.
D	8' 11-3/4"	*Add for high-polish finish*	9,300.
D	8' 11-3/4"	†Figured Sapele	89,500.
D	8' 11-3/4"	†Kewazinga Bubinga	93,400.
D	8' 11-3/4"	†East Indian Rosewood	103,100.
D	8' 11-3/4"	†Santos Rosewood	102,400.
D	8' 11-3/4"	†Macassar Ebony	114,200.
D	8' 11-3/4"	†Hepplewhite Dark Cherry	96,400.

*For explanation of terms and prices, please see pages 29–34.

Model	Size	Style and Finish	Price*

Story & Clark

Factory-installed Pianomation system (CD-ROM or 3.5" floppy) with Orchestration and Record options, add from $4,900 to $5,600, depending on model. Not available factory-installed on 44" vertical. Already included in 4' 7" and 5' 1" grands.

Verticals

Model	Size	Style and Finish	Price
American	42"	Oak	3,790.
American	42"	Cherry	3,790.
Century	42"	Italian Provincial Walnut	3,790.
Chippendale	42"	Chippendale Oak	4,190.
Chippendale	42"	Chippendale Cherry	4,190.
Heirloom	42"	Queen Anne Oak	3,790.
Heirloom	42"	Queen Anne Oak	3,790.
Mediterranean	42"	Mediterranean Oak	3,790.
Southwest	42"	French Provincial White	3,790.
Prelude	44"	Continental Polished Ebony	2,590.
Prelude	44"	Continental Polished Mahogany	2,590.
Church	46"	Ebony	4,390.
Church	46"	Oak	4,390.
Church	46"	Cherry	4,390.
Church	46"	Walnut	4,390.
School	46"	Ebony	4,390.
School	46"	Oak	4,390.
School	46"	Cherry	4,390.
School	46"	Walnut	4,390.

Grands

Model	Size	Style and Finish	Price
SC407	4' 7"	Polished Ebony with Pianomation	14,740.
SC501	5' 1"	Polished Ebony with Pianomation	15,910.
Hampton	5' 5"	Ebony	20,000.
Hampton	5' 5"	Cherry	20,000.
Hampton	5' 5"	Walnut	20,000.

Strauss

Verticals

Model	Size	Style and Finish	Price
UP-108	42"	Continental Polished Ebony	2,398.
UP-108	42"	Continental Polished Mahogany	2,398.

Model	Size	Style and Finish	Price*
UP-108	42"	Continental Polished Walnut	2,398.
UP-108	42"	*Continental Polished White*	2,498.
UP-110	43"	Continental Polished Ebony	2,500.
UP-110	43"	Continental Polished Mahogany	2,500.
UP-110	43"	Continental Polished Walnut	2,500.
UP-110	43"	*Continental Polished White*	2,598.
UP-117C	46"	Chippendale Polished Ebony	2,598.
UP-117C	46"	Chippendale Polished Mahogany	2,598.
UP-117C	46"	Chippendale Polished Walnut	2,598.
UP-117C	46"	*Chippendale Polished White*	2,698.
UP-117D	46"	Polished Ebony	2,598.
UP-117D	46"	Polished Mahogany	2,598.
UP-117D	46"	Polished Walnut	2,598.
UP-117D	46"	*Polished White*	2,698.
UP-120	48"	Polished Ebony	2,798.
UP-120	48"	Polished Mahogany	2,798.
UP-120	48"	Polished Walnut	2,798.
UP-120	48"	*Polished White*	2,898.
UP-130	52"	Polished Ebony	3,490.
UP-130	52"	Polished Mahogany	3,490.
UP-130	52"	Polished Walnut	3,490.
UP-130	52"	*Polished White*	3,598.
Grands			
GP-170	5' 5"	Polished Ebony	8,000.
GP-170	5' 5"	*Polished Mahogany*	8,000.
GP-170	5' 5"	*Polished Walnut*	8,000.
GP-170	5' 5"	*Polished White*	8,000.

Walter, Charles R.

Verticals

1520	43"	Oak	6,724.
1520	43"	Cherry	6,954.
1520	43"	Walnut	6,984.
1520	43"	Mahogany	7,090.
1520	43"	Riviera Oak	6,700.
1520	43"	Italian Provincial Oak	6,728.

*For explanation of terms and prices, please see pages 29–34.

Model	Size	Style and Finish	Price*

Walter, Charles R. (continued)

Model	Size	Style and Finish	Price*
1520	43"	Italian Provincial Walnut	6,986.
1520	43"	French Provincial Oak	6,980.
1520	43"	French Provincial Walnut	7,184.
1520	43"	French Provincial Cherry	7,186.
1520	43"	Country Classic Oak	6,760.
1520	43"	Country Classic Cherry	6,900.
1520	43"	Queen Anne Oak	7,050.
1520	43"	Queen Anne Cherry	7,250.
1520	43"	Queen Anne Mahogany	7,250.
1500	45"	Ebony	6,540.
1500	45"	Polished Ebony	6,856.
1500	45"	Oak	6,280.
1500	45"	Walnut	6,540.
1500	45"	Mahogany	6,644.
1500	45"	Gothic Oak	6,660.

Grands

Model	Size	Style and Finish	Price*
W190	6' 4"	Ebony	29,000.
W190	6' 4"	Semi-Polished Ebony	29,600.
W190	6' 4"	Mahogany	30,200.
W190	6' 4"	Semi-Polished Mahogany	30,600.
W190	6' 4"	Walnut	30,200.
W190	6' 4"	Semi-Polished Walnut	30,600.
W190	6' 4"	Cherry	30,200.
W190	6' 4"	Semi-Polished Cherry	30,600.
W190	6' 4"	Chippendale Mahogany	31,200.
W190	6' 4"	Chippendale Semi-Polished Mahogany	31,600.
W190	6' 4"	Chippendale Cherry	31,200.
W190	6' 4"	Chippendale Semi-Polished Cherry	31,600.

Weber

Verticals

Model	Size	Style and Finish	Price*
W-40	42-1/2"	85-note Continental Polished Ebony	4,100.
W-109	43"	Continental Polished Ebony	3,380.
W-41A	43"	Continental Polished Ebony	4,200.
W-41A	43"	Continental Walnut	4,460.

Model	Size	Style and Finish	Price*
W-41A	43"	Continental Polished Walnut	4,460.
W-41A	43"	Continental Polished Mahogany	4,460.
W-41A	43"	Continental Polished Brown Mahogany	4,460.
W-41A	43"	Continental Polished Ivory	4,240.
W-41A	43"	Continental Polished White	4,240.
WF-41	43"	Cherry	4,600.
WF-41	43"	Mediterranean Oak	4,700.
WF-41	43"	French Provincial Cherry	4,700.
WFX-43	43-1/2"	French Cherry	5,120.
WFD-44	44-1/2"	Mahogany	5,500.
WFD-44	44-1/2"	Oak	5,500.
WFD-44	44-1/2"	French Provincial Cherry	5,500.
W-45C	45"	Chippendale Polished Mahogany	5,780.
WC-46	46"	Continental Polished Ebony	5,180.
WC-46	46"	Continental Polished Mahogany	5,320.
WC-46	46"	Continental Polished Walnut	5,320.
WS-46	46"	American Oak	5,180.
WS-46	46"	American Walnut	5,180.
W-121	48"	Polished Ebony	4,460.
W-48	48"	Ebony	5,800.
W-48	48"	Polished Ebony	5,800.
W-48	48"	Walnut	6,060.
W-48	48"	Polished Walnut	6,060.
W-48	48"	Polished Mahogany	6,060.
W-48	48"	Polished Brown Mahogany	6,060.
W-53	52"	Polished Ebony	6,600.
W-53	52"	Polished Mahogany	6,880.

Grands

Model	Size	Style and Finish	Price*
WG-50	4' 11-1/2"	Ebony	11,180.
WG-50	4' 11-1/2"	Polished Ebony	11,180.
WG-50	4' 11-1/2"	Walnut	11,920.
WG-50	4' 11-1/2"	Polished Mahogany	11,920.
WG-50	4' 11-1/2"	Polished Brown Mahogany	11,920.
WG-50	4' 11-1/2"	Cherry	11,920.
WG-50	4' 11-1/2"	Polished Ivory	11,580.
WG-50	4' 11-1/2"	Polished White	11,580.
WG-50	4' 11-1/2"	Queen Anne Polished Ebony	13,120.

*For explanation of terms and prices, please see pages 29–34.

Model	Size	Style and Finish	Price*
Weber (continued)			
WG-50	4' 11-1/2"	Queen Anne Polished Mahogany	13,620.
WG-50	4' 11-1/2"	Queen Anne Polished Brown Mahogany	13,620.
WG-50	4' 11-1/2"	Queen Anne Cherry	13,780.
WG-50	4' 11-1/2"	Queen Anne Polished Ivory	13,620.
WG-50	4' 11-1/2"	Queen Anne Polished White	13,620.
WG-51	5' 1"	Ebony	12,200.
WG-51	5' 1"	Polished Ebony	12,200.
WG-51	5' 1"	Walnut	12,740.
WG-51	5' 1"	Polished Walnut	12,740.
WG-51	5' 1"	Polished Mahogany	12,740.
WG-51	5' 1"	Polished Brown Mahogany	12,740.
WG-51	5' 1"	Cherry	12,740.
WG-51	5' 1"	Polished Ivory	12,640.
WG-51	5' 1"	Polished White	12,640.
WG-57	5' 7"	Ebony	14,260.
WG-57	5' 7"	Polished Ebony	14,260.
WG-57	5' 7"	Walnut	14,860.
WG-57	5' 7"	Polished Walnut	14,860.
WG-57	5' 7"	Polished Mahogany	14,860.
WG-57	5' 7"	Polished Brown Mahogany	14,860.
WG-57	5' 7"	Cherry	14,860.
WG-57	5' 7"	Polished Ivory	14,660.
WG-57	5' 7"	Polished White	14,660.
WG-60	6' 1"	Ebony	15,160.
WG-60	6' 1"	Polished Ebony	15,160.
WG-60	6' 1"	Polished Ivory	15,760.
WG-70	7'	Ebony	23,500.
WG-70	7'	Polished Ebony	23,500.
WG-90	9'	Ebony	46,760.
WG-90	9'	Polished Ebony	46,760.

Weinbach

Note: Prices below do not include bench. Add from $220 to $630 (most are under $400), depending on choice of bench.

Verticals

Model	Size	Style and Finish	Price*
104-III	42"	Continental Polished Ebony	4,700.
104-III	42"	Continental Polished Walnut	4,700.
104-III	42"	Continental Polished Flame Mahogany	4,700.
114-I	45"	Demi-Chippendale Polished Walnut	5,500.
114-I	45"	Demi-Chippendale Pol.Flame Mahogany	5,500.
114-IC	45"	Chippendale Polished Walnut	5,780.
114-IC	45"	Chippendale Polished Flame Mahogany	5,780.
114-II	45"	Polished Ebony	4,780.
114-II	45"	Polished Walnut	4,780.
114-II	45"	Polished Flame Mahogany	4,780.
114-IV	45"	Polished Ebony	5,180.
114-IV	45"	Polished Walnut	5,180.
114-IV	45"	Polished Flame Mahogany	5,180.
124-II	50"	Polished Ebony	6,180.
124-II	50"	Polished Walnut	6,180.
124-II	50"	Polished Flame Mahogany	6,180.

Grands

Model	Size	Style and Finish	Price*
155	5' 3"	Polished Ebony	16,380.
155	5' 3"	Polished Walnut	16,380.
155	5' 3"	Polished Flame Mahogany	16,380.
170	5' 8"	Polished Ebony	17,580.
170	5' 8"	Polished Walnut	17,580.
170	5' 8"	Polished Flame Mahogany	17,580.
192	6' 4"	Polished Ebony	20,180.
192	6' 4"	Polished Walnut	20,180.
192	6' 4"	Polished Flame Mahogany	20,180.

Wurlitzer

Verticals

Model	Size	Style and Finish	Price*
1175A	37"	Country Oak	3,390.
1176N	37"	Queen Anne Cherry	3,390.
2270A	42"	Ribbon-Striped Mahogany	3,780.

*For explanation of terms and prices, please see pages 29–34.

Model	Size	Style and Finish	Price*

Wurlitzer (continued)

Model	Size	Style and Finish	Price*
2275B	42"	Country Oak	3,780.
2276B	42"	Queen Anne Cherry	3,780.
2277S	42"	Queen Anne Scrubbed Oak	3,780.

Grands

Model	Size	Style and Finish	Price*
C143	4' 7"	Ebony	10,080.
C143	4' 7"	Polished Ebony	10,080.
C143	4' 7"	Polished Mahogany	10,400.
C143	4' 7"	Polished Oak	10,400.
C143	4' 7"	Polished White	10,080.
C153	5' 1"	Ebony	11,680.
C153	5' 1"	Polished Ebony	11,680.
C153	5' 1"	Polished Mahogany	12,080.
C153	5' 1"	Walnut	12,080.
C153	5' 1"	Oak	12,080.
C153	5' 1"	Polished Ivory	11,680.
C153QA	5' 1"	Queen Anne Polished Mahogany	14,080.
C153QA	5' 1"	Queen Anne Oak	14,080.
C153QA	5' 1"	Queen Anne Cherry	14,080.
C173	5' 8"	Ebony	12,880.
C173	5' 8"	Polished Ebony	12,880.
C173	5' 8"	Polished Mahogany	13,280.
C173	5' 8"	Polished White	12,880.

Yamaha

Acoustic Verticals

Model	Size	Style and Finish	Price*
M1F	44"	Continental Ebony	5,390.
M1F	44"	Continental Polished Ebony	5,490.
M1F	44"	Continental American Walnut	5,590.
M1F	44"	Continental Polished Mahogany	6,790.
M1F	44"	Continental Polished White	6,690.
M450	44"	American Oak	3,590.
M450	44"	Cherry	3,590.
M500C	44"	Cottage Cherry	4,590.
M500CM	44"	Country Manor Light Oak	5,890.

Model	Size	Style and Finish	Price*
M500CV	44"	Country Villa White Oak	6,090.
M500F	44"	Florentine Light Oak	4,590.
M500G	44"	Georgian Mahogany	5,490.
M500H	44"	Hancock Brown Cherry	4,390.
M500M	44"	Milano Dark Oak	4,590.
M500P	44"	Parisian Cherry	5,690.
M500QA	44"	Queen Anne Cherry	4,790.
M500S	44"	Sheraton Mahogany	4,390.
P22T	45"	American Walnut	4,790.
P22T	45"	Black Oak	4,790.
P22T	45"	Dark Oak	4,790.
P22T	45"	Light Oak	4,790.
P2F	45"	Continental Polished Ebony	5,890.
P2F	45"	Continental Polished Mahogany	6,990.
U1S	48"	Ebony	7,190.
U1S	48"	Polished Ebony	7,290.
U1S	48"	American Walnut	7,590.
U1S	48"	Polished American Walnut	8,190.
U1S	48"	Polished Mahogany	8,190.
WX1S	48"	Polished Ebony	9,490.
U3S	52"	Polished Ebony	9,690.
U3S	52"	Polished Mahogany	10,790.
WX7S	52"	Polished Ebony	12,990.

Disklavier Verticals

Model	Size	Style and Finish	Price*
MX80A	44"	Continental Polished Ebony	9,466.
MX80A	44"	Continental American Walnut	9,390.
MX80A	44"	Continental Polished Mahogany	10,590.
MX80A	44"	Continental Polished White	10,490.
MX85CM	44"	Country Manor Light Oak	9,990.
MX85CV	44"	Country Villa White Oak	10,190.
MX85G	44"	Georgian Mahogany	9,590.
MX85P	44"	Parisian Cherry	9,790.
MX85QA	44"	Queen Anne Cherry	8,890.
MX88	45"	Walnut	9,286.
MX88	45"	Oak	9,286.
MX88	45"	Black Oak	9,286.
MX88	45"	Light Oak	9,286.

*For explanation of terms and prices, please see pages 29–34.

Model	Size	Style and Finish	Price*
Yamaha (continued)			
MX100IIXG	48"	Polished Ebony	12,890.
MX100IIXG	48"	American Walnut	13,218.
MX100IIXG	48"	Polished Mahogany	13,790.
MX100IIXG	48"	Polished White	13,080.
Silent Verticals			
MP50C	44"	Cottage Cherry	6,790.
MP50CM	44"	Country Manor Light Oak	8,258.
MP50CV	44"	Country Villa White Oak	8,470.
MP50F	44"	Florentine Light Oak	6,790.
MP50G	44"	Georgian Mahogany	7,834.
MP50H	44"	Hancock Brown Cherry	6,590.
MP50M	44"	Milano Dark Oak	6,790.
MP50P	44"	Parisian Cherry	8,046.
MP50QA	44"	Queen Anne Cherry	6,990.
MP50S	44"	Sheraton Mahogany	6,590.
MP51	44"	Continental Polished Ebony	7,690.
MP100	48"	Polished Ebony	9,424.
Silent Disklavier Verticals			
MPX100IIXG	48"	Polished Ebony	13,950.
MPX100IIXG	48"	American Walnut	14,484.
MPX100IIXG	48"	Polished White	14,306.
Acoustic Grands			
GP1	5' 3"	Polished Ebony	11,990.
GH1B	5' 3"	Ebony	12,990.
GH1B	5' 3"	Polished Ebony	13,290.
GH1B	5' 3"	American Walnut	14,790.
GH1B	5' 3"	Polished American Walnut	14,790.
GH1B	5' 3"	Polished Mahogany	14,790.
GH1B	5' 3"	Polished Ivory	14,790.
GH1B	5' 3"	Polished White	14,390.
C1	5' 3"	Ebony	16,790.
C1	5' 3"	Polished Ebony	17,090.
C1	5' 3"	American Walnut	19,290.
C1	5' 3"	Polished Mahogany	19,990.
C1	5' 3"	Polished White	19,290.

Model	Size	Style and Finish	Price*
C2	5' 8"	Ebony	19,090.
C2	5' 8"	Polished Ebony	19,390.
C2	5' 8"	American Walnut	21,990.
C2	5' 8"	Polished Walnut	22,690.
C2	5' 8"	Polished Mahogany	21,990.
C2	5' 8"	Polished White	20,790.
C3	6' 1"	Ebony	26,190.
C3	6' 1"	Polished Ebony	26,390.
C3	6' 1"	American Walnut	28,990.
C3	6' 1"	Polished Mahogany	29,390.
S4	6' 3"	Polished Ebony	47,390.
C5	6' 7"	Ebony	28,290.
C5	6' 7"	Polished Ebony	28,490.
C6	6' 11"	Ebony	31,390.
C6	6' 11"	Polished Ebony	31,590.
S6	6' 11"	Polished Ebony	53,590.
C7	7' 6"	Ebony	35,790.
C7	7' 6"	Polished Ebony	35,990.
CFIIIS	9'	Polished Ebony	97,990.

Disklavier Grands

Model	Size	Style and Finish	Price*
DA1 IIXG	4' 11"	Polished Ebony	24,030.
DGP1XG	5' 3"	Polished Ebony (playback only)	19,538.
DGP1 IIXG	5' 3"	Polished Ebony	22,998.
DGH1BXG	5' 3"	Polished Ebony (playback only)	20,830.
DGH1BIIXG	5' 3"	*Ebony*	23,990.
DGH1BIIXG	5' 3"	Polished Ebony	24,290.
DGH1BIIXG	5' 3"	American Walnut	25,710.
DGH1BIIXG	5' 3"	*Polished American Walnut*	25,790.
DGH1BIIXG	5' 3"	*Polished Mahogany*	25,790.
DGH1BIIXG	5' 3"	*Polished Ivory*	25,790.
DGH1BIIXG	5' 3"	Polished White	25,390.
DC1 IIXG	5' 3"	*Ebony*	27,790.
DC1 IIXG	5' 3"	Polished Ebony	28,090.
DC1 IIXG	5' 3"	*Polished American Walnut*	31,790.
DC1 IIXG	5' 3"	*Polished Mahogany*	30,990.
DC1 IIXG	5' 3"	*Polished Ivory*	30,790.
DC1 IIXG	5' 3"	*Polished White*	30,290.

*For explanation of terms and prices, please see pages 29–34.

Model	Size	Style and Finish	Price*

Yamaha (continued)

Model	Size	Style and Finish	Price*
DC2 IIXG	5' 8"	*Ebony*	30,090.
DC2 IIXG	5' 8"	Polished Ebony	30,390.
DC2 IIXG	5' 8"	American Walnut	32,910.
DC2 IIXG	5' 8"	*Polished American Walnut*	33,690.
DC2 IIXG	5' 8"	*Polished Mahogany*	32,990.
DC2 IIXG	5' 8"	Polished White	31,790.
DC3 IIXG	6' 1"	*Ebony*	37,190.
DC3 IIXG	6' 1"	Polished Ebony	37,390.
DC3 IIXG	6' 1"	American Walnut	39,990.
DC3 IIXG	6' 1"	*Polished Mahogany*	40,390.
DC5 IIXG	6' 7"	Ebony	39,290.
DC5 IIXG	6' 7"	Polished Ebony	39,490.
DC6 IIXG	6' 11"	Ebony	42,390.
DC6 IIXG	6' 11"	Polished Ebony	42,590.
DC7 IIXG	7' 6"	Ebony	46,790.
DC7 IIXG	7' 6"	Polished Ebony	46,990.

Silent Grands

Model	Size	Style and Finish	Price*
A1S	4' 11"	Polished Ebony	20,064.
C1S	5' 3"	Polished Ebony	21,794.
C2S	5' 8"	Polished Ebony	24,084.
C3S	6' 1"	Polished Ebony	31,058.

Young Chang

Verticals

Model	Size	Style and Finish	Price*
U-107A	42"	Continental Ebony	5,100.
U-107A	42"	Continental Polished Ebony	5,100.
U-107A	42"	Continental Walnut	5,280.
U-107A	42"	Continental Polished Walnut	5,280.
U-107A	42"	Continental Polished Red Mahogany	5,280.
U-107A	42"	Continental Polished Oak	5,280.
U-107A	42"	Continental Polished Ivory	5,240.
U-107A	42"	Continental Polished White	5,240.
E-102	43"	Continental Polished Ebony	4,200.
E-102	43"	Continental Polished Walnut	4,460.
E-102	43"	Continental Polished Red Mahogany	4,460.

Model	Size	Style and Finish	Price*
E-102	43"	Continental Polished Brown Mahogany	4,460.
E-102	43"	Continental Polished Oak	4,460.
E-102	43"	Continental Polished Ivory	4,240.
E-102	43"	Continental Polished White	4,240.
E-109	43"	Continental Polished Ebony	3,380.
U-109C	43"	Queen Anne Polished Ebony	5,300.
U-109C	43"	Queen Anne Polished Walnut	5,460.
U-109C	43"	Queen Anne Polished Red Mahogany	5,460.
F-108B	43-1/2"	Mahogany	4,940.
F-108B	43-1/2"	Italian Provincial Walnut	4,940.
F-108B	43-1/2"	Mediterranean Oak	4,940.
F-108B	43-1/2"	Queen Anne Oak	4,960.
F-108B	43-1/2"	Queen Anne Cherry	5,120.
F-108B	43-1/2"	French Provincial Cherry	5,120.
F-116	46-1/2"	Mediterranean Oak	5,600.
F-116	46-1/2"	Italian Provincial Walnut	5,600.
F-116	46-1/2"	French Provincial Cherry	5,740.
U-116	46-1/2"	Ebony	5,180.
U-116	46-1/2"	Polished Ebony	5,180.
U-116	46-1/2"	American Walnut	5,320.
U-116	46-1/2"	American Oak	5,320.
U-116	46-1/2"	Polished Oak	5,320.
U-116S	46-1/2"	American Walnut (School)	5,180.
U-116S	46-1/2"	American Oak (School)	5,180.
E-118	47"	Polished Ebony	4,060.
U-121	48"	Ebony	5,860.
U-121	48"	Polished Ebony	5,860.
U-121	48"	Walnut	6,120.
U-121	48"	Polished Walnut	6,120.
U-121	48"	American Oak	6,120.
U-121	48"	Polished Oak	6,120.
U-121	48"	Polished Brown Mahogany	6,120.
U-121N	48"	Polished Ebony	4,460.
U-131	52"	Ebony	6,600.
U-131	52"	Polished Ebony	6,600.
U-131	52"	Walnut	6,880.
U-131	52"	Polished Walnut	6,880.

*For explanation of terms and prices, please see pages 29–34.

Model	Size	Style and Finish	Price*

Young Chang (continued)

Grands

Model	Size	Style and Finish	Price*
G-150	4' 11-1/2"	Ebony	11,180.
G-150	4' 11-1/2"	Polished Ebony	11,180.
G-150	4' 11-1/2"	American Walnut	11,900.
G-150	4' 11-1/2"	Polished Red Mahogany	11,920.
G-150	4' 11-1/2"	Polished Brown Mahogany	11,920.
G-150	4' 11-1/2"	Polished Oak	11,920.
G-150	4' 11-1/2"	Polished Ivory	11,580.
G-150	4' 11-1/2"	Polished White	11,580.
G-150	4' 11-1/2"	Queen Anne Polished Ebony	13,120.
G-150	4' 11-1/2"	Queen Anne Polished Red Mahog.	13,620.
G-150	4' 11-1/2"	Queen Anne Polished Oak	13,620.
G-150	4' 11-1/2"	Queen Anne Cherry	13,780.
G-150	4' 11-1/2"	Queen Anne Polished Ivory	13,360.
G-150	4' 11-1/2"	Queen Anne Polished White	13,360.
G-157	5' 2"	Ebony	12,360.
G-157	5' 2"	Polished Ebony	12,360.
G-157	5' 2"	Walnut	12,860.
G-157	5' 2"	Polished Walnut	12,860.
G-157	5' 2"	Polished Red Mahogany	12,860.
G-157	5' 2"	Polished Brown Mahogany	12,860.
G-157	5' 2"	Polished Oak	12,860.
G-157	5' 2"	Polished Ivory	12,760.
G-157	5' 2"	Polished White	12,760.
G-157D	5' 2"	Country French Oak	15,640.
G-157D	5' 2"	Country French Cherry	15,940.
G-157D	5' 2"	Queen Anne Red Mahogany	15,640.
G-157D	5' 2"	Queen Anne Cherry	15,940.
G-175	5' 9"	Ebony	14,560.
G-175	5' 9"	Polished Ebony	14,560.
G-175	5' 9"	Walnut	15,160.
G-175	5' 9"	Polished Walnut	15,160.
G-175	5' 9"	Polished Red Mahogany	15,160.
G-175	5' 9"	Polished Brown Mahogany	15,160.
G-175	5' 9"	Polished Oak	15,160.
G-175	5' 9"	Polished Ivory	14,960.

Model	Size	Style and Finish	Price*
G-175	5' 9"	Polished White	14,960.
G-175D	5' 9"	Empire Inlaid Polished Brown Mahog.	17,640.
G-185	6' 1"	Ebony	15,160.
G-185	6' 1"	Polished Ebony	15,160.
G-185	6' 1"	Walnut	15,840.
G-185	6' 1"	Polished Walnut	15,840.
G-185	6' 1"	Polished Red Mahogany	15,840.
G-185	6' 1"	Polished Ivory	15,760.
PG-185	6' 1"	Ebony	15,960.
PG-185	6' 1"	Polished Ebony	15,960.
G-208	6' 10"	Polished Ebony	19,180.
G-213	7'	Ebony	23,500.
G-213	7'	Polished Ebony	23,500.
G-275	9'	Ebony	46,760.
G-275	9'	Polished Ebony	46,760.

*For explanation of terms and prices, please see pages 29–34.